all
things
to
all
people

all things

to all people

A Primer for K–12 ESL Teachers in Small Programs

Donald N. Flemming
Lucie C. Germer
Christiane Kelley

Teachers of English to Speakers of Other Languages, Inc.

Typeset in Palatino and Antique Olive by
World Composition Services, Inc., Sterling, Virginia
and printed by
Pantagraph Printing, Bloomington, Illinois USA

Copyright © 1993 by Teachers of English to Speakers of Other Languages, Inc. (TESOL).

All rights reserved. Copying or further publication of the contents of this work are not permitted without permission of TESOL, except for limited "fair use" for educational, scholarly, and similar purposes as authorized by U.S. Copyright Law, in which case appropriate notice of the source of the work should be given.

Helen Kornblum *Director of Communications and Marketing*
Marilyn Kupetz *Senior Editor*
Ellen Garshick *Copy Editor*
David Connell *Illustrator*

Teachers of English to Speakers of Other Languages, Inc.
1600 Cameron Street, Suite 300
Alexandria, VA 22314 USA
Tel 703-836-0774 • Fax 703-836-7864

ISBN 0-939791-44-7
Library of Congress Catalog No. 92-63213

dedication

This primer is dedicated to the many students and their families who made it possible, and necessary, for us to be all things to all people.

"I feel as though I am in the middle of a web of responsibilities—a three-dimensional web that could only be represented pictorially with computer graphics."

Lucie, September 1988

table of contents

Introduction 1
Chapter 1 The ESL Program 6
Chapter 2 The Students 36
Chapter 3 Student Life Outside the Classroom 44
Chapter 4 The Student and the School 56
Chapter 5 Families 78
Chapter 6 Teachers in the Mainstream 104
Chapter 7 Administrators, or Who Is My Boss, Anyway? 132
Chapter 8 Nurses and Guidance Counselors 152
Chapter 9 Sponsors: Pros and Cons 166
Chapter 10 Function and Identity: I Teach; Therefore, I Am 176
Postscript 194
References 197

Appendix A Parent's Handbook   199
Appendix B Competencies for ESL Teachers   211
Appendix C Glossary of Technical Terms   213
Appendix D Selected Bibliography   219
About the Authors   223

acknowledgments

The field of second language pedagogy in the United States is an area of tremendous activity and productivity. We acknowledge our debt to the many writers and thinkers who have inspired our own professional growth over the years. The most important of these influences are listed in Appendix D.

We would like to single out for thanks those who have assisted us in the preparation of this book. Foremost is Dr. Richard Yorkey, currently in active retirement following a long career as an ESL teacher, writer, and professional leader. We are deeply grateful for his thoughtful and detailed comments on our developing manuscript. We also extend our appreciation to the anonymous reviewers on the TESOL editorial board, whose support for and constructive critiques of our manuscript made it possible to bring this project to fruition. Our thanks to Professor Jack Richards, Chair of the TESOL Publications Committee; to Helen Kornblum, Director of Marketing and Communications at TESOL; to Marilyn Kupetz, Senior Editor; and to Ellen Garshick, who as copy editor made every effort to correct our sins of omission and commission.

introduction

Purpose

This primer describes the comprehensive nature of the duties of professionals who work directly with children from non-English backgrounds in the public schools of the United States. Teachers of English as a second language (ESL) in the public schools are called on to play many roles, yet most Americans, including educators, have no idea what ESL teachers do. We have spent many years attempting to describe the job as we have come to understand it and believe that our insights will prove useful to others. Teachers new to the ESL field will find in this book a careful description of what it is like to be responsible for the education of language minority students. Furthermore, a better understanding of the ESL teacher's role will not only lead to greater support and appreciation for a valuable team member but help administrators and others who come in contact with language minority students and their families to carry out their responsibilities.

Audience

We hope everyone who works in the ESL field will find this primer useful. However, although we as ESL teachers must be all things to all people, as the title of this book claims, a book such as this cannot. The text is designed primarily to help newcomers to the ESL field to understand the profession they have chosen. In particular, we have geared the book toward those educators who work in school districts having small numbers (30 or fewer) of limited English proficient students[1] from a variety of linguistic backgrounds. The text may also be helpful to ESL associates, aides, and volunteer tutors as well as to administrators, guidance counselors, health professionals, secretaries, and mainstream teachers, including specialists who have or may someday have language minority children in their classrooms. Furthermore, this primer provides an excellent basis for either preservice or in-service staff training.

Setting

There are several million recent immigrants in the United States, and according to Olsen's (1991) survey more than 2 million of the newcomers are school-age children. Many have settled in urban areas because of family contacts or job opportunities, but scattered across the country are many thousands of children, though often only a handful of any particular ethnic group, who attend public schools in suburban and rural settings. Our intent is to provide support to the educators who work with language minority students in these suburban and rural schools.

We make the distinction between the urban setting on one hand and suburban or rural settings on the other because the typical approach in an urban setting with a large non-English-background school population is to teach self-contained classes: the teacher stays in the same room all day, as the students often do. The more proficient students may leave the ESL classroom to attend other classes for one or more periods per day. There are often several ESL teachers in the school (or school system) and, in some cases, bilingual educators as well.

The ESL instructor often speaks the native language of the language minority students.

In contrast, in suburban and rural settings the total population of language minority students will number only from 10 to 30.[2] These students will be distributed—by no means equally—among all levels and throughout district school buildings. Although some districts attempt to centralize the program by creating "magnet" schools, many ESL teachers feel that they must have an itinerant operation, traveling to two or more buildings to meet with individuals or groups on site.

Even with small numbers of students, the age range is always great—normally from 5 to 18. Previous schooling, concept development, and language proficiency also vary. This heterogeneity means that the typical ESL class may consist of very few students, perhaps only one. Generally, only at the high school level can a group of six to eight students receive simultaneous instruction.

ESL teachers in most suburban and rural programs function sometimes as resource persons to whom students go during certain periods each day and sometimes as "doctors" making "house calls," who visit their clients on site to work with them on the particular task of the moment.

The nature and size of the student population make for an unusual teaching situation. The ESL teacher is challenged by program mobility, integration with the mainstream program, scheduling, and programming of individualized instructional activities. These challenges, coupled with the many nonacademic responsibilities that arise, mean that ESL teachers must indeed fulfill many roles as they attempt to serve their student population.

Structure

Each of the 10 chapters that make up this primer deals with a topic that is central to the professional activity of the ESL teacher. The chapters contain an overview of each topic as well as illustrative anecdotes, which are designed not only to evoke vividly the experiences of the ESL teacher but to present the issues in context so that they may be held up for examination and reflection. They are a window through which the reader can view the world of ESL. In contrast to the narrative sections, which define what should be, the anecdotes describe what is. In this way we hope to provoke a process of analysis that, though it may lead to conclusions different from ours, will contribute to the reader's personal and professional growth. In fact, our discussions during the preparation of this book have fostered our own development in many ways. To help in that process of analysis, we pose key questions at the beginning of each chapter. Readers should keep the questions in mind while reading the chapter with a view toward seeking answers as they study the material.

Sources

The material presented here is based on our collective wisdom and experiences. We have collaborated continuously for many years and have spent the past 3 years in frequent consultation as we developed, revised, and edited the manuscript. Although we have taken our anecdotes from real-life situations, we have made every attempt to mask the identities of the individuals originally involved. In fact, no person should believe that any character depicted in this text refers specifically to her or him.

All the individuals mentioned are fictitious; we invented them by forming composite prototypes.

Our experience has taught us that representatives of all cultures can exhibit both positive and negative behaviors depending on their personal circumstances at a given moment. To the extent that our comments focus on the negative aspects of the behavior of individuals from one ethnic background or another, we categorically state that we are not interested in either the creation or perpetuation of stereotypes. The situations described are designed solely to focus on issues that come before professionals dealing with language minority students. By reflecting on these behaviors and attempting to analyze them in context, we believe, ESL teachers can come up with responses that are in the best interests of the students and their families.

Notes

1. The federal government uses the term *limited English proficient* to classify children who need special English language training. We believe that this term lends itself to negative interpretations and to classifying those who need to improve their English language skills as somehow inferior to those who learned English as their mother tongue. Thus in most cases we employ the more neutral *language minority* students.
2. Although federal laws require special language instruction for all language minority students incapable of achieving at grade level in English-only classes, when the number of such students drops below 10, most districts try to handle this special instruction by using Chapter I teachers, classroom aides, and volunteer tutors rather than by employing a full-time ESL teacher. We should add that part-time ESL teachers are not uncommon.

chapter one

The ESL Program

What Is ESL?
FOCUSING QUESTIONS

★ What does an ESL teacher do?
★ What are the objectives of an ESL program?
★ How are these objectives realized?
★ How are ESL programs attached to the rest of the curriculum?
★ What are the components of the ESL curriculum?
★ How are students enrolled in ESL programs?
★ How are daily schedules arranged?
★ Where does ESL instruction take place?

Just what is English as a second language? Do you as an ESL teacher know what your subject matter is? Is it a subject matter? You must be able to respond intelligently to these questions, as you will be asked them continually. If you say you teach English, a response that seems easy and noncontroversial, you will get into trouble with all but the most passive interrogators. If you teach English, how does your program differ from the language arts in the primary grades or the English classes at the secondary level? Yes, you do teach English, but . . . .

You must come up with a brief and comprehensible definition of the academic core of your program. After giving this concise response to inquiring parties, you must quickly add that your professional responsibilities include many services other than direct instruction in language skills and that, if the questioner is truly interested, you will provide a detailed job description. In short, you need to demonstrate control of your function by being able to articulate readily the kind of response your colleagues and the public expect to hear. At the same time, you must be careful not to minimize or trivialize your role by inadvertently communicating the idea that teaching language skills in some sort of remedial fashion is *all* that you do.

ESL programs have two basic goals: to develop the English language skills of language minority students to the point where they have educational opportunity equal to that of their U.S.-born counterparts, and to develop the students' knowledge of and skills in cultural patterns in the United States so that they can function in an integrated and rewarding fashion in U.S. society.

To achieve these goals, ESL programs typically articulate a set of specific objectives:

1. To develop the English language proficiency of the students to a level at which they understand and are understood in common social and academic settings. This proficiency includes satisfactory pronunciation and intonation, adequate control of vocabulary, and sufficient grammatical accuracy to prevent miscommunication.
2. To develop a control of basic concepts that will allow for

learning in the content areas: language arts, social studies, science, and math.
3. To facilitate the socialization and acculturation process by integrating language minority students and their English-speaking peers into extracurricular activities.
4. To integrate language minority students into the mainstream classroom program. This process is gradual and does not necessarily move at the same rate in each content area for each individual.
5. To develop the learning strategies and classroom behaviors that are necessary for academic success in the U.S. public school system.

Given these goals and objectives, what does the typical ESL program look like? ESL programs vary widely, especially the small programs described here. Some have a language orientation, with an emphasis on the development of skills such as listening comprehension, speaking, reading, and writing (vocabulary, grammar, and culture are usually considered underlying knowledge necessary for the development of these skills). Other programs are content-based, developing language skills through the study of subject matter, such as economics or American studies.

In spite of the wide variation in ESL programs, certain elements characterize many of the programs familiar to us. To begin with, the ESL program is typically an appendix to the standard curriculum—an add-on to meet what many school principals perceive as a temporary need or a crisis requiring ad hoc intervention. In general, you will not be assigned to a particular classroom or even to one specific building. You typically report not to a department head or principal but to an assistant superintendent. The program has a certain degree of independence from the mainstream activities, a condition with both advantages and disadvantages. On the plus side, you have more freedom to plan curriculum, carry out instructional activities, and evaluate your program than most of your colleagues do. On the downside, the lack of a home in both the physical and organizational senses sometimes means that you struggle for instructional space and lack administrative support when you need it for one reason or another.

The ESL curriculum, in keeping with the goals delineated above, centers on the language spoken in the United States and on the cultures of those who speak it. In the very early stages of instruction, the language needed for "survival" is taught—the words and phrases students need to make it through the school day. Correspondingly, the initial lessons in culture have to do with how to behave in a U.S. school. From these basic concepts, the language program expands by adding sentence complexity, incorporating study of the terminology used in academic settings, and developing concepts for satisfactory performance in the content areas. Cultural studies move from a focus on the classroom to a focus on the individual, the family, and the community, to work and leisure activities, and then to social and political structures.

What does a typical program look like? How is the schedule set up? How many students are dealt with at one time? How are groups chosen? Will you ever work in a mainstream classroom, or are students always pulled out for ESL instruction? All of these questions are interrelated and must be considered when drawing up a schedule. The process works like this: You, as the ESL teacher, calling on others as necessary, identify the potential clients for the ESL program based on (a) carryover from the previous year, (b) new registrants, and (c) referrals by mainstream teachers of students who were not identified earlier. Second, you test or somehow evaluate the English proficiency level of each student. With the list of all potential clients and their ability range, you analyze the grade levels and the buildings in which these students have been placed. You then consult the schedule for each potential client and determine which period(s) might be available for ESL instruction. Using four variables (grade level, proficiency, building, and schedule), you construct a schedule that maximizes your assistance to the group as a whole.

The logistics make compromises unavoidable. Sustained, intensive language instruction is crucial to bring about proficiency in the academic aspects of English, but often 30 minutes per day is all you can arrange for some language minority students. Schedule conflicts and time lost traveling among buildings make alternatives impossible.

Here is a typical daily schedule:
7:30–8:25   American History and Culture
8:25–9:15   Advanced ESL—high school
9:20–10:10 Beginning ESL—high school
10:10–10:25 Planning, paperwork, consultations—high school
10:25–10:35 Travel from high school to junior high
10:35–11:25 Individual tutoring—junior high

11:25–11:35 Travel from junior high to elementary school
11:35–12:00 Planning, consultations, paperwork
12:00–12:30 Individual tutoring—third grader
12:30–1:10 Lunch and planning; meetings with other teachers
1:10–1:40 Second grade
1:40–2:10 Tutoring one or two fourth graders
2:10–2:40 Pre-first and first grade class

It is rare for a class to number more than eight students. You will hold many sessions with only one or two individuals. Although this pattern lowers your productivity, the personal attention students receive increases instructional effectiveness considerably.

Most typically you will pull a student out of the mainstream classroom for ESL instruction. However, if you, as the staff member working on ESL with a particular child, are an aide or a tutor (as opposed to a certified teacher), or if the child strongly resists leaving the regular classroom, you occasionally provide support instruction in the child's homeroom by helping the student to complete activities assigned by the mainstream teacher.

Learning Activities: From TPR to the TOEFL

FOCUSING QUESTIONS

★ What methods and techniques are common in ESL programs?

★ What kind of English must be taught in ESL programs?

★ What might a Whole Language reading lesson look like?

★ What is the relative importance of the phonics and "sight word" approaches in an ESL program?

★ Why is it important for ESL teachers to share their writing with their students?

★ How can dialogue journals contribute to a writing program?

★ How does student motivation affect the teacher's choice of activities?

★ What is the role of culture in an ESL program?

★ Should an ESL teacher give grades?

Like all second language instructors, you will use a number of strategies to develop your students' language skills. In the early stages of instruction, Total Physical Response (TPR) (Asher, 1982) will figure prominently. In TPR the teacher gives oral commands to the learners, who demonstrate comprehension by carrying out the commands. The commands range from such simple instructions as "stand up" and "sit down" to much more complex commands such as, "If there is a girl with a red dress seated at the right side of the table, take your notebook and place it under her chair." TPR fits nicely into the second language acquisition theory articulated by Krashen (1982). Based on his theoretical work, Krashen and Terrell (1983) have developed a method of teaching second languages called the *Natural Approach.* The essence of this method is to surround the learners with language they can understand, assuming that the formula *exposure + comprehension* will automatically lead to acquisition. The language input can take many forms: teacher talk, classroom labels, audiovisual presentations, wall charts, books and other print materials, group discussions, and guest speakers. Your function at all times is to make certain the students comprehend the language to which they are exposed. Since the Natural Approach is really not a method but a set of beliefs about how learners acquire languages, you are free to use any techniques that seem to produce the desired learning outcomes.

One popular strategy is cooperative learning groups: you give two or more students a task and instruct them to complete it by working together. Both formal research and anecdotal evidence indicate that the peer tutoring that occurs during cooperative learning produces results far beyond those achieved when only the teacher is involved in directing an activity.

Still another common procedure is to use what is called

sheltered English, usually in conjunction with a program of content-based instruction. In these programs, you analyze the material being studied in the mainstream content areas (language arts, social studies, mathematics, and science) and prepare lesson plans that simplify the language used to present the concepts. You might also use more visuals or hands-on materials than are provided in the regular classroom. Because it involves making content area material comprehensible to the language minority student, sheltered English meshes nicely with the principles of the Natural Approach.

The books and materials you select will vary according to your language teaching philosophy, but those who subscribe to the Natural Approach typically use authentic materials, such as printed texts written for nonacademic purposes: signs, instructions, recipes, schedules, magazines, and newspapers, as well as literature of all types. You will select and use print materials and audiovisual aids to produce the learning outcomes identified earlier in this chapter.

Because concept development is a key objective, you will make certain to use materials that systematically present the notions your clients need to master in order to function in the U.S. school system. Language minority children often come to school without knowing some concepts that are basic for English-speaking Americans: color differentiation, sizes, shapes, family relationships, spatial relationships, number systems, time measurement, and others. And even when the students know the concepts, they most likely do not know the English labels for them. Material that teaches these concepts becomes the core of the initial instructional program.

What kind of English must be taught and learned in the ESL program? Cummins (1989) has identified two types of language that school children must use. *Conversational* or *surface-level* language is the type of language people use in everyday interaction. The words are basic, the sentences short, and the variety limited, but it works. Most children learn this type of language readily, often without formal instruction. Laypersons and ingenuous educators often believe that children who can converse effectively in English on the playground must be fluent enough to handle the mainstream curriculum. However, wrote Cummins, another type of language, called *academic language proficiency,* is the language required for academic success. It includes knowledge of the concepts, vocabulary, and grammar typically taught and tested (or otherwise graded) in the U.S. classroom. Children do not acquire academic language from playmates, nor do they acquire it casually; it must be taught or, better said, opportunity must be provided for the student to learn it. This requirement and the need to facilitate the acculturation or at least the cross-cultural understanding of students from non-English backgrounds justify the existence of a special program known as English as a second language.

In addition to the distinction made by Cummins, other factors affect second language acquisition in the public school setting. Scarcella (1990) discusses these factors thoroughly; here we outline the essential points, which can be summed up as attitude, aptitude, motivation, and methodology.

Although it is not clear what teaching behaviors influence learners' attitudes toward language, the following hypothesis seems reasonable: if you have a positive attitude toward minority languages and cultures, your students will as a result be inclined to have a positive attitude toward the English language and U.S. culture. The question of aptitude is controversial, but whether or not researchers can agree on differences in language learning ability, consensus does seem to exist on the issue of learning styles. Recognizing that your students will have a variety of preferences with regard to learning modes, you will want to plan your activities accordingly. Motivation, whether extrinsic or intrinsic, will play an important role in your program. As you think about motivation, you need to consider the importance of your students' feelings and emotions and how they affect the students' readiness and willingness to participate in the learning activities. Last, you must be knowledgeable about the results of second language acquisition research so that you can avoid activities that are either counterproductive or simply time wasters. You need to know what experienced teachers have found to be the most productive second language teaching approaches and how you can modify them to fit your own teaching style and your students' learning styles.

With attitude, aptitude, motivation, and methodology firmly in mind, you can begin to make intelligent choices about methods, materials, and techniques. All have the same objective: to develop the students' English language skills until they can function at grade level in the mainstream classroom. To realize this objective, you must be able to assess accurately each student's proficiency, to diagnose individual strengths and weaknesses, and to use the resulting information in planning learning activities.

Your training and subsequent professional activity have made you aware of appropriate methods and techniques that are most likely to bring about timely growth in your students' language proficiency. For example, you will probably use the Whole Language approach in teaching reading, incorporating both standard literary texts and multicultural folk tales into your program. You will use a process approach in teaching writing, including such key components as peer response groups, individual conferences, in-house publishing of student writings, and dialogue journals.

I have seven beginning readers at the elementary school: two kindergartners, one in pre-first grade, and one in third. Because I see them in three groups, it is hard to pull them all together, but last week's lesson worked beautifully. For the city/farm focus of the week I'd brought in a library book about a little boy looking for eggs on his grandma's farm (Campbell, 1983). It's a predictable book, and every page has a fold-up flap under which you can find the animal the little boy asked for eggs. Everyone loved the book and began to chant the chorus by the second repetition. After a few days, I made up some dittoed sheets with a picture of the boy and the words "Buster asked the . . . " on one side and "Oh, dear! No eggs here!" at the bottom of the other side. Each of the children made a page for our book, with a drawing of an animal and a construction paper flap. The third grader made the final page, in which the boy asked the hen for an egg. Turn over flap one and you see the hen, then lift up the hen and there are the eggs. All the children signed their pages, I put them together, and we had a new book.

None of that is especially exciting, but what has impressed me is what has happened since. Every day in each group the children have grabbed both books and "read" them, one after another. Some days they've asked me to read one or both of the books; other days they've "read" to each other. One of the first graders said that he likes the library book better—but only because it has a better binding. He thinks we ought to get better bindings for our book. As the children go through their book, they identify each picture with its author and comment on the pictures. One kid's drawing of two ducks is "wicked good," and another's rabbit looks like the one in the classroom down the hall. Another's, the third grader's, whose imagination is not bounded by mundane concerns, has a lovely unicorn hiding behind a bush. Once, when we went through the book, I asked what noise each animal made, and the unicorn stumped them until the littlest child of all said, "I know what noise unicorn make. Honk! Honk!"

What I mainly understand from this experience is that these kids need much more repetition than we think. They went through one version or another of the story about Buster and the eggs at least 10 times in the past week. I also observed that the students are now using patterns spontaneously, are writing books following the model, and are showing genuine enthusiasm for books and for reading.

Even a simple book like that one can give all kinds of opportunities for cultural understanding. The Southeast Asian children and I had a discussion of the fact that, although Americans eat hen's eggs but not usually duck eggs, duck eggs are perfectly good to eat. With Moslem children the picture of the pig would give a great opening for discussion of who eats pork and why. The book ends with Buster finding "two eggs for breakfast," but when the children "read" the book, they usually said the eggs were for lunch or supper, so we talked about that, too.

Besides, now I know what kind of noise a unicorn makes!

In the teaching of reading, many mainstream teachers are firm believers in the value of phonics—in spite of the widespread acceptance of the Whole Language approach in the language arts profession at large and among ESL teachers. Although possibly of some value to native speakers, phonics may be counterproductive when used with second language learners. The rationale is simple enough: phonics is based on prior knowledge of the standard pronunciation of the English words used in the text to be studied. ESL students do not have this prior knowledge! Even without having studied linguistics, which is generally the core of the ESL teacher's professional training, the mainstream teacher should be able to comprehend that phonics is not appropriate for the language minority population.

21
The ESL Program

Chapter 1

After considerable thought, I decided that if the mainstream teachers are going to use phonics, we'd better do some basic work on distinctions between sounds. (Do they do this in all the standard classrooms, or do they assume everyone can hear the distinctions?) I have a series of big minimal-pair flip charts that an artist friend did for her ESL teacher husband, with one distinction to a page, three pictures for each sound (kick-cake, pill-pail), and a different geometric shape for each vowel sound. I've been using these with the kindergartners, the first graders, and the third grader who has problems reading. I correlate sound with shape—the triangle words and the square words. Each child has a chance to identify words by sound as I say them, and one other child is the checker, whose job is to say either "good job" or "try again" to the "star of the show." That leaves only one child who isn't directly involved, and the third one usually is busy outguessing the other two as we go through the exercise.

I'm trying to prepare them for success in their regular classrooms even if I don't agree with the type of success. I've been bothered because the elementary school is being dragged kicking and screaming from phonics to Whole Language. Some of the teachers would like to do a lot of Whole Language whereas others feel threatened by it. Even the ones who like it seem to feel that it isn't really language arts, just a bit of dessert for the children who do their short vowels right.

So much of what we do is instinctive. I have no proof that minimal-pair drills will help the children with their phonics.

The ESL Program

But it seems logical; if their attention is focused on distinguishing sounds and connecting them to something they already know, then it should be easy to transfer this knowledge to the letters they're learning how to make. How would I prove it? Why should I bother? They enjoy the game; they've learned some new vocabulary; they're practicing certain social skills (wait your turn, listen to your neighbor). A lot of my early training was in conducting drills like these, but because I've been more interested in suprasegmentals than in segmentals,[1] I haven't worked much with students on distinguishing sounds. The kids love it, and I'm interested to see if it helps them in their decoding skills. We'll see what happens.

Today I have to give three cheers to Sylvia Ashton-Warner. One activity that I do is straight out of her book (1963)—a sight-word vocabulary-building technique. I have all the students (from third grade down) tell me any word they want to learn. All the students have their own colored felt-tip markers, and every day we write the new words on flash cards. Then I ask the students to read me some of the words from the previous days. If they can't read any given word, I tear up the card and tell them (following Ashton-Warner) that we got rid of it because it wasn't important to them. Ashton-

Warner claims that any word a child cares about will be learned on the spot.

Today one of my kindergartners, who had absolutely refused to play the game, had to go for an inoculation. On returning, he took a card and asked me how to write *shot*. We wrote it, and he promptly read it back to me several times. Maybe it's too soon to be certain, but I'll bet he knows that word tomorrow and the next day and the next. I wonder what the next word he cares about will be?

I'm finally doing some role playing. Wow! The students are really excited about it. I hadn't done any for a long time. I'm doing it with a group of advanced students using a business story text (Costello, 1987). A couple of the students had business interests, so it fit right in. The students love it because it's related to real life and the roles are quite meaty. The students all have had jobs, so they know the kinds of decisions and situations portrayed in the book are realistic. The role plays are challenging too; the students have to opt for competition or cooperation. They love to be hard on each other. Somebody's going to come away the winner and somebody's going to come away the loser, or maybe they're going to work it out to everyone's advantage. This activity does require good reading skills, but the interest level is high, and role playing is a great motivator. We go over a lot of the vocabulary ahead of time, so the students have a fairly solid base to build on. And we follow up the role play with a discussion of the issues involved. All in all, I think it's great. I'm having fun; they're having fun. I bought the book at the beginning of the year and sat on it waiting for the chemistry to be right. Things finally came together last week.

I do find it frustrating sometimes year after year never to be able to say, "This is my ESL syllabus for my advanced students." This time, by imposing on them something they like, I'm giving some structure to my course and I think I'm seeing a lot of progress in their oral skills too. Role on!

I scored more than two points when I made *that* basket! I guess I've believed that teachers should write in writing class ever since I started learning about process writing, but I haven't always done it. Sometimes I have sat there, guilt ridden but immobile, and watched the students struggle to write a few words on the hostile blank page, but of late I have begun to write every time I ask the students to do so. Today I was struggling with a piece that wasn't was working, so I rolled the paper up into a ball and threw it into the wastebasket. I hadn't really planned to do it for effect, but wow! Did I get reactions! First the students all laughed, and then we had a very good discussion about what happens when writers get into trouble. We all shared the strategies we have developed to deal with writer's block or lesser obstacles such as structural or sequencing problems. It was clear to me that they benefited from knowing that becoming a writer is a process that goes on forever. They appreciated the fact that I was providing an honest model. They didn't say so, but it was obvious. I think I've atoned for some of my guilt. The students are very forgiving in any case.

Dialogue journals don't always work, but sometimes they do. They weren't going anywhere with a couple of my high school boys—or, I should say, the boys weren't going anywhere with them. In any case, about a week ago one student was complaining that he never had any dates even though he knows a lot of other guys are going out on weekends. As a lark I said to the other boy, "How do *you* ask a girl for a date?" He replied that he'd just broken up with his girlfriend, but that it didn't matter because there were plenty of girls around. His advice was pretty straightforward: "Ask the girl what she's doing Friday night, and then ask her to go to the movies." I said that sounded like pretty good advice and asked the dateless one what he thought. He didn't say much, so we went on to something else.

Today the student came in, grabbed his journal, and started writing before I had a chance to introduce my first activity. When he finished, he handed the journal to me and said, "First you write in it, then he writes in it." He wanted both me and his ad hoc courtship counselor to respond to his entry. Guess what he wrote! That's right, he took our advice and got himself a date, and I got myself a three-way dialogue journal. Not bad!

Why is it that we always strive to do a better job when new eyes are watching us? A fifth grader wanted to bring his friend to class today, and I couldn't see any reason to say no. I prepared a special lesson, one that the friend could take part in, and we got to work. But it was all play for the visitor, who had a great time—I suppose because it was a change from his routine.

I've been doing a lot of work with folk tales lately, but I had to think of something "macho" so my student wouldn't be embarrassed. I settled on "Jack and the Beanstalk," and after reading it we had a great discussion about laziness, magic, the triumph of good over evil, and so on. Then we played a game of concentration using the vocabulary from the story. My student is very good at concentration, so winning made him feel on a par with his friend. I let the game go on longer than I probably should have, but they were having so much fun, and I rationalized that José was learning lots of useful vocabulary.

What I've learned from these visits is that peers are very important to a student's success. My student's American friend really wants him to master English. In his own naive way, the friend helps him all the time. This caring makes my student a receptive learner. He's on his way.

---- ★ ----

In addition to the language skills you are trying to teach, you also need to think about motivation. Many factors affect motivation: personal goals, emotional state, self-esteem, physical condition, engagement with lesson content, prior learning, relations with peers, attitude toward the teacher, and others. Many of these factors are beyond your control, but you must try to deal with them if learning is to take place. You should keep in mind that all learning is subjective; the learners must take ownership of the learning activity before intellectual growth can occur.

--- ★ ---

I tried something in the ESL room in the high school. I put up a graffiti board, one of those boards you use a marker on, with an attached marker and an eraser. The students asked me what it was for, and I told them they could write anything on it that they wanted but that obscenities had to be written in their native languages because the board is visible from the hall. I wouldn't give them any more direction than that.

It's been interesting. Everyone except my new Vietnamese student has written on it, and my oldest student is the only one who has written only in English. We've had messages in Spanish, French, and Greek plus a couple of drawings. The first three messages, two in Greek and one in Spanish, all dealt with friendship, even though none of the students knew what the others had written when they chose their phrases. One boy has used it to flirt with a girl (in French and mangled Spanish), and one guy wrote one day when he was sick, "I'm not here today."

I've also used it for reminders to the students and for my own comments. Like so many of the things I do, I'm not sure what the pedagogical value is, but it seems to be important to the students.

--- ★ ---

A ninth grade student who had spent 5 years in a small private school was very confident in the beginning weeks of the school year. Around Christmas she began asking me if I couldn't help her with her spelling. I put her off until second semester because before that there was no time in my schedule. The first week of the second semester I looked at an English paper. As I suspected, at least half of the red marks pertained to usage errors. As I go back to her tomorrow with a grammar workbook, I wonder how she'll take to it.

Is she really ready to tackle tense and modality? Her sister at the middle school told me she didn't think I needed to come anymore. This was after I stopped helping her so much with her spelling sentences (she was trying to use two to three spelling words in the same sentence) and discussing her writing (which is very imaginative) and attempted to attack the perfect (tense). I am going to work on it a bit more, but if I don't see much progress, I'll drop it. After 5 years of working with ESL students and verbs, I know that one can only support the acquisition process, not force it!

P.S. She wasn't ready. She doesn't see the need yet.

★

When my high school students came in today, I knew the lesson plan was out the window. There are always signs—some obvious, some more subtle. I noticed no one had the book we've been reading. I didn't see any ESL notebooks either. (I make them have special three-ring binders to hold all the things we do: vocabulary, cultural units, grammar points, compositions, dialogue journals, and so on.) The students' conversation had to do with an upcoming test in history class. I pretended I didn't know what was going on and started to introduce my lesson, but no one was paying attention. They were doing their best to continue the conversation about history. I paused and glared at them. Silence. I asked what was going on. Silence. Then I asked, "Would you like to talk about your history test?" and the room started to boil. They opened their books, they fired questions at me, they condescendingly shouted answers to each other before I had half a chance to formulate a response. I tried to bring order to this historic chaos. After class, I checked my lesson plans. "See if students have read the story." "Try to get a discussion going." Really!

It seems that the kids' need for attention to their content-area work tends to come in waves. I'm hoping that by keeping a careful log of these events I'll be able to figure out how that wave pattern works. Why is it that for several days running they are perfectly happy to deal with whatever curriculum *I* come up with, and then suddenly it seems that no matter what period of the day they're coming in, they all have papers, assignments, or something they must get done right away?

They immediately adopt a behavior that suggests they've never even heard of what we were doing before. No matter what a great lesson I have come up with, no matter what *my* inclinations, it's time to do the social studies report, do the oceanography project, or write up the biology lab. And the moods come in waves!

---   ★   ---

You should try to take advantage of the cultural diversity your students represent and to select materials for learning activities according to the ethnic makeup of the class. Culture should be everywhere: on the bookshelves, on the walls, on your desk. There should be frequent celebrations based on holidays around the globe. Visitors should come in to talk about their group's customs and folkways. You should lead discussions of the current events in the countries of origin of the immigrant students, and students should be encouraged to recite stories or anecdotes they recall from their native lands. But at the same time you should plan and present a full schedule of activities based on the culture of the United States, and assist other teachers in making the mainstream classes more multicultural while stressing acculturation to U.S. society in your own program. To this end, you should also invite representatives of the local community to make guest presentations: police officers, fire fighters, and others.

Chapter 1

---★---

*I*f you want to become an expert in geopolitics, become an ESL teacher. I've had to learn about countries I barely knew existed. I certainly didn't know anything meaningful even if I could, by chance, locate them on a map. But I soon learned that my students, especially the older ones, are quite well informed about the current political scene in their countries of origin. They would put their U.S.-born counterparts to shame. Not that everything they know is correct or without bias, but their interest and their curiosity are impressive.

One of the high school kids brought in a videotape on recent events in Cambodia. The kids were fascinated by the film even though it was incredibly grisly. I learn a lot from the kids just by observing the way they deal with things. They seem to take a very calm view of death—almost stoical, one might say. I ask myself, "To what extent are they still emotionally tied to Indochina?" I think some of them would like to be able to help Cambodia solve its problems, but most of their dreams are linked to the past. Nonetheless, I think they are beginning to understand the power of an education. Maybe their concern for justice in their homeland will be the motivation they need to continue their studies.

---★---

You should be concerned with the development of the whole person and thus give much attention to what may seem to be extraneous activities. But in spite of these unavoidable diversions, you must never lose sight of your objectives. To remind the students that they also have goals to meet, you should use a grading system. All grading systems are subjective, so you should not apologize for evaluating your students essentially on effort invested in assigned activities rather than on mastery of any particular linguistic structures. You must argue that your high school students' ESL study should count toward graduation, much as foreign language study counts for U.S.-born students.

★

I've been griping about how others grade their students, and I started feeling somewhat uneasy. I decided I'd better try to clarify how *I* come up with grades. After all, I'm subject to all the pitfalls that snare the colleagues I constantly criticize. How *do* I grade students?

I don't know if there is any subject or skill area that one can say contains a concrete body of material to be mastered, thus lending itself to a relatively objective evaluation on an absolute scale. If there is, ESL surely isn't one of them. What I do is to try to establish a kind of base from which the students depart each quarter and then attempt to determine the progress they have made starting from that point. It wouldn't be fair to grade them on their overall proficiency, first, because many factors beyond the classroom contribute to linguistic growth and, second, because proficiency is not necessarily related to classroom performance. But I hate to use such simplistic rating devices as averages of vocabulary quiz scores or listening comprehension exercises and the like, and I do like to give some reward for effort.

---★---

You should assist those students interested in going on to college to prepare for the standardized English language proficiency test called the TOEFL (Test of English as a Foreign Language).[2] In addition, you should help all students as they prepare their work for their mainstream teachers. Although you should not see your role as that of offering remedial instruction, both the ESL students and their mainstream teachers will expect you to perform this service. The plus side of this obligation is that you will be able to assess the ability (or lack thereof) of the ESL student to carry out assigned tasks in the mainstream classroom. In this way you can make decisions on allowing ESL students to exit from the program with some degree of assurance.

What is ESL? It is a specially designed program to help children from linguistic minority groups develop their English language skills and cultural knowledge about the United States. The objective of an ESL program is to prepare these students to function at grade level in the mainstream classroom. In addition to the core program, you will be responsible for a myriad of other academic and social services.

Notes

1. Suprasegmentals refer to intonation; segmentals, to pronunciation.
2. Administered to nonnative speakers of English, the TOEFL is produced and scored by Educational Testing Service, Princeton, NJ.

chapter two

The Students

FOCUSING QUESTIONS

★ What kinds of students does one find in ESL programs?

★ What attitudes do language minority parents have toward schooling?

★ What variation does the ESL teacher find in the student population?

Who are the ESL teacher's clients in the U.S. public schools? Not surprisingly, in a country composed of people from dozens of ethnic backgrounds, the students who need special instruction in the English language, as well as many other academic and social support services—ESL students, bilinguals, limited English proficient students, language minority children, refugees, migrants, illegal immigrants—come from every part of the globe and from a broad spectrum of economic backgrounds, with all the attendant variation in physical, emotional, and intellectual development. Even in rural areas of the United States the diversity of the origins of even small numbers of students from non-English backgrounds is impressive.

As in the cities, the bulk of the linguistic minorities in nonmetropolitan areas represent recent immigrant groups. As of the early 1990s schools were registering ESL students from three main regions: Southeast Asia, Eastern Europe, and Latin America (including Mexico and the Caribbean). The students speak a wide variety of languages and dialects, many of which are unknown to U.S. school personnel. Some have arrived after facing the horrors of war and political repression or of seeing loved ones tortured and murdered.

---------- ★ ----------

I have a first grade boy from Cambodia. His family, including uncles, aunts, and grandmother, is intact. The nuclear family lives in a house they're buying, complete with a microwave oven and a dog named Lassie, plus some chickens that peck around the front dooryard. The boy is a beautiful child with chubby cheeks and eyelashes that go on forever. He's soft-spoken in any language.

A new fourth grader just arrived from Germany. Born to an American mother and a German father, she speaks English and German but reads and writes only German. The mother is sure that the child is ahead of her U.S.-born peers because of the superiority of her German education. The child babbles continuously, trying to make sense of her new life, and is quite leery of trying to read or write in English for fear of making mistakes. She enjoys reading her language experience stories, though. Her classroom teacher is sure that no progress will occur until she studies phonics.

One of my fourth graders, also Cambodian, is not so fortunate. His father is dead, and his mother has survived as best she can. Unfortunately her behavior has caused conflicts with just about every other Cambodian woman in town. This poor boy is troubled by the lack of a father and by his mother's behavior; to make matters worse, he is aware that he is not as bright as his classmates. But he wants very badly to be a good citizen. He doesn't act out or get surly the way some of his classmates do. He just gets silly.

José is in second grade. He and his mother are Spanish; she married a U.S. serviceman who brought them both back to the States. His mother is caught between wanting him to learn English as fast as possible and not wanting to lose the one person she knows in town who speaks Spanish with her accent. Sometimes she speaks Spanish with him; then, feeling guilty, she insists on their speaking English, providing him with a model of reversed nouns and adjectives, final -s where no English speaker would put it, and *b*'s and *v*'s doing unusual things. José is a bright child, and his mother will be easy to work with. All she needs is reassurance that the best thing she can do is use Spanish with him while letting him know that she's glad he knows English, too.

I have a Taiwanese girl in eighth grade. Her family moved here recently to open a Chinese restaurant. She lived in another state for a while, and there she was kept in fourth grade for 3 years because she's so short. She's very smart and highly motivated, and will be fun to work with.

And now a few words about my high school group: a Vietnamese girl, sponsored by a local church group, has experienced considerable culture shock, which has been complicated by the fact that she has missed a good deal of schooling because she had to stay home to care for the younger children while her mother worked. Now her older brother seems to be angry because he has to work while she gets an education rather than caring for him.

At the high school I'll be working with a Salvadoran girl. Her aunt, who brought her in, told me, "She says she wants to work in a factory, but we think she is smart enough to go on to college. She just doesn't have enough self-confidence." It's great to have the *family* pushing education.

A Cambodian boy is my only high school holdover from last year. Both parents are dead; he made it through the Khmer Rouge and the camps with his sister and her husband. He has a part-time job and takes the classes he needs to get his diploma. He's also fighting the aftereffects of tuberculosis. I worry about him.

——————— ★ ———————

Some students are here on international exchanges, the sons and daughters of wealthy families who want their children to learn English for the status and the professional opportunities such knowledge brings. Because most of these students are from affluent families, they tend to be bright and academically oriented. They are also well behaved except when they get homesick; then they show their adolescent colors.

——————— ★ ———————

The principal thought up a special course for the exchange students—a kind of survey of U.S. culture—and I just love it! I include all of my non-English-background high school kids as well, and we have a great time. I'm learning as much about pop culture as they are. Fortunately, I have two teenagers at home who provide me with authentic data for my lesson plans.

Another benefit of the special course (which I keep to myself) is that this class makes it look as if I have a reasonable course load. It's good PR for both me and the school.

★

Some language minority students have never been in a school before in spite of their advanced age. Some are top-notch students, highly literate in their mother tongue. Some have parents who value education for all their children. Other parents believe schooling is worthwhile for males only; for them the school serves as a protective holding tank for daughters until they are marriageable. Some parents send their children to school on a regular basis; others often keep them home to look after younger siblings. Some parents take an active interest in the school life of their children. Others seem to fear the school, to be in awe of the staff, and, as a result, to shy away from contact.

Diverse origins, values, capabilities, and needs characterize the ESL teacher's clientele, and the kaleidoscopic configuration of the student body does not stop there. You must also deal with constant change in student enrollment. Daily attendance varies, and the continual arrivals and departures of ESL students present special challenges. Many students appear on opening day in the fall, and some of them will still be in your classes the following June, but the constant migration of recent immigrants, motivated by a variety of factors, results in programmatic instability and shortfalls in learning outcomes.

In addition to what may be called the *external*, or externally imposed, differentiation, the same variation exists among individuals in the ESL population as is found among native English-speaking students. ESL students range in age from 5 to 21, and their presence in the public schools depends on their mental abilities and the generosity of the school district. (Some districts have free public kindergarten or Head Start programs; others do not. Federal law requires schools to work with children between the ages of 3 and 21 if they have learning deficiencies.)

Some students have severe emotional problems resulting from trauma or other causes and find the school routine impossible to carry out in a nondisruptive fashion. Some manifest constant or frequent anger and are hostilely aggressive in their relations with others. Others, passive to the point of being withdrawn, are unresponsive to teacher requests and spend much of their time lost in thought. Others need only to learn English so that they can function within the mainstream curriculum. They come to class regularly, are always friendly and cooperative, learn quickly, are fond of teaching their peers, and appear to be adjusting well to their new life in the United States.

Who are the ESL students? The students themselves might

well answer that question with the song title, "We Are the World," and they would be right. Many ESL classrooms or, better said, programs are microcosms of the global situation. Therefore, like the international diplomat, you must be prepared to deal with constant variation and change. You must be creatively flexible.

chapter three

Student Life Outside the Classroom

FOCUSING QUESTIONS

★ What are the families of language minority children like?

★ What relationships do language minority children have with English-speaking children?

★ What social institutions serve to maintain ethnic identity?

★ What problems of social adjustment do language minority children encounter?

★ How do exchange students differ from those whose families have immigrated to the United States?

★ How do the experiences of language minority children in the home or neighborhood affect their schooling?

As noted in chapter 2, students come from a wide variety of family backgrounds. The families of the more or less permanent immigrant population represent every type imaginable: intact nuclear families, extended families, single-parent families, mixed families, and other, looser, groupings usually involving some blood relationships as well as friendship bonds.

---⭐---

"*I* am so happy. I am so happy. I am so happy." One of my Vietnamese girls couldn't say anything else today, and after I'd explained to the rest of the class, they beamed with her. She found out last night that her father and four siblings are due to arrive next week and, in a separate call, that her mother and two sisters have definitely escaped from Vietnam and are safe in Malaysia. She couldn't work or do anything today. She just sat there glowing.

---⭐---

Immigrant families must deal with a complex bureaucracy whose tolerance for their English language deficiencies is minimal. As a result, they often come to depend on their children in the public schools for support in a variety of ways. Quite commonly, for instance, children as young as 7 or 8 years old are called on to provide all the care of their younger siblings: dressing brothers and sisters in the morning, feeding them, and then undressing and putting them to bed at night. It also means that if there is a need to watch over a young child during the day, the slightly older sibling will be required to stay home from school and provide day care.

Equally common is a dependence on the school children as interpreters and translators. Children are required to accompany parents and other family members on trips to government and social agencies, where it is their responsibility to communicate with the bureaucrats assigned to the particular function. The children must not only be absent from school but face a great challenge, as many of the concepts they must deal with are both foreign to them and above their level of intellectual development. An additional negative outcome is that they are often forced to see their parents or other family members lose face when they are treated in an undignified fashion by agency officials. The fact that the children have a certain power as a result of their growing proficiency in English, combined with the loss of dignity on the part of parents who cannot stand up to affronts by U.S. social workers, leads to a breakdown of discipline and cultural loyalty and may contribute to family dissolution.

Immigrant children are somewhat sheltered in their earlier years from contacts with the English-speaking world. Social interaction tends to be limited to family and to other members of the particular ethnic group.

---★---

Sometimes I wonder about the acculturation process. When I was in Mexico for Peace Corps training, it seemed that I was able to make friends easily with both sexes. Maybe this ability is culture specific. Anyway, my Cambodian boys don't seem to have any U.S.-born friends. They just hang around together and don't show much interest in developing new relationships. On weekends, I gather they continue this pattern. They travel to other communities for celebrations and get-togethers and relate only to males of the same cultural background. As with the U.S.-born students, there are social norms that they follow—manner of dress, style of hair, etc. Their common appearance seems to give them a sense of group identity while setting them apart from their U.S.-born peers. My Cambodian girls, on the other hand, seem to mix well with their U.S.-born classmates. I haven't seen any evidence of their dating non-Cambodians, but maybe they do so in groups.

Should I be concerned about the lack of relationships between my Cambodian students and their U.S.-born peers? Does my role as a teacher of U.S. culture include social engineering? Can these kids become truly integrated in our society without intimate relations with Americans? Are parental fears of assimilation a factor here?

─────── ★ ───────

Often a regional religious organization serving the ethnic minority is the focus of interaction for the immigrants and provides a site for ceremonies and celebrations of all kinds, allowing for maintenance of language and traditions. At these events the older children tend to be paired off, either at their initiative or, depending on the ethnic group, by the parents of the couple in question. Thus, endogamy, or marriage within the group, is still the norm in many immigrant communities.

Outside the Classroom

---- ★ ----

I have to help my students sort out their feelings about the topic of the hour: marriage and courtship. The kids talk about it all the time—both boys and girls to varying degrees—because more and more of the girls either are being approached by families, have become engaged, or are soon to be engaged. Some have staved off several requests so far but may not be able to much longer. The boys are suddenly thinking more about relationships, or someone in the family or an older friend has recently married, is getting married, or is pursuing someone. There's tremendous discussion all the time. It's never-ending.

---- ★ ----

Sometimes the love affairs will present you with more serious challenges.

---- ★ ----

One of my high school boys is in a bad mood. His girlfriend tried to commit suicide on Sunday, which is why he wasn't in school yesterday. I didn't ask for too many details, partly because I'm never sure whether to believe him and partly because in this context the causative details aren't important. I don't really care why the girl took two bottles of Tylenol. What I care about is that my student was shaking and saying he didn't know how much more he could take, that he felt guilty, and that he was exhausted because he'd been out of town all night (maybe). I told him I was no expert on suicide and tried to steer him toward the high school psychologist (he refused) and the Samaritans[1] (he took the number). All I could do for him was to tell him I thought he could survive this, too, that I was mad at his girlfriend because she had done this, and that it wasn't his fault. Anyhow, after he'd told me more about it and talked about his own suicide attempt a few years ago, he finally said "thanks," and we went back into the classroom.

---- ★ ----

Romantic problems are universal, but other adjustments seem tied to U.S. culture. It does not take the language minority students long to develop an enthusiasm for U.S. toys and technology. Most have access to television and thus are fully informed about the latest fashions in pseudo weaponry or games of imaginary (it is hoped) violence. Science fiction and comic strip characters as well as rock stars and TV personalities soon become a part of the students' repertoire.

As the students move up the age ladder and become teenagers, they want to trade in their skateboards for a "set of wheels." You may find yourself helping a student struggle through the rules-of-the-road manual. You will feel the anxiety build as the day of the license examination approaches, and you will share the joy or sorrow as the results become known. But the hand-holding doesn't stop there; the student may have brushes with the law, and you may need to explain what the guilty party (your ESL student) must do to redeem himself. There may be trips to police stations (but, Officer . . .) and sometimes court appearances at which you will have to translate legalese into Basic English.

---------★---------

Today I heard voices as I came up to the door of my room. My first thought was that one of the students had flipped out and was talking to himself, but as I went in, another student announced that he didn't have a pass to show me because he hadn't been to the office yet, but that he had to talk to me. I had to go talk to his counselor, he said, because he was really in trouble now. The police were after him. They said he'd stolen something. I asked noncommittally, "Did you?"

"What do you think? It was some cigarettes, some papers, a passport, from the glove compartment of a guy from my country." He said he hadn't done it; he had been at home and asleep for 2 hours when the items were stolen. I promised to talk with his counselor, and as the bell rang, he and the other boy got up to leave.

"They can't do anything to me. They can't prove it."

From the depths of his experience, the other kid said, "You

want to bet? They can arrest you and take you to court, and you'll have to pay."

"I can't pay. I'm broke." And the accused one smiled a desperately brave, macho smile.

---★---

To court with my oldest student, who has managed to parlay a relatively minor traffic violation into a real problem with the law. He was supposed to have some papers regularized before driving again but didn't, so the government sent him a notice in official-ese to suspend his license. He didn't understand it, so he put it in his glove compartment. Apparently he never thought of showing it to any of the Americans he knows, so it looked very bad when the police caught him. The prosecutor feels that my student understands what is going on and is just trying to manipulate the system. This guy could not successfully manipulate his way across the room, but he did understand enough of what was going on to ask for a lawyer. Was this sort of task in my job description?

The refugee coordinator called to say that my student had been convicted, had to pay court costs, and had to spend 2 or 3 days in jail. I stopped by his house after school, but he wasn't there. Later, the prosecutor called both me and the refugee coordinator. He agreed to let my student off the hook as he obviously doesn't understand English. Whew!

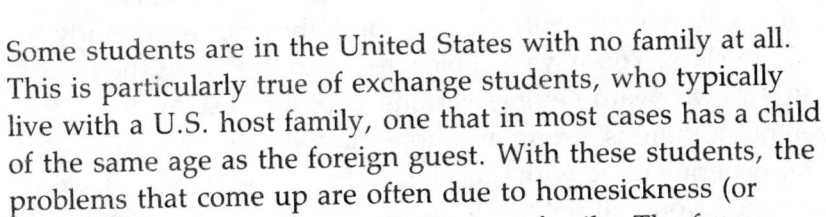

Some students are in the United States with no family at all. This is particularly true of exchange students, who typically live with a U.S. host family, one that in most cases has a child of the same age as the foreign guest. With these students, the problems that come up are often due to homesickness (or culture shock) or conflicts with the host family. The former typically dissipates on its own as the exchange student makes new friends and has positive experiences in the new culture.

Conflicts with the host family, which are often more problematic than those resulting from culture shock, are nearly always due to faulty communication between the parties either before or during the visit. Misunderstandings occur and hostility begins to develop. Sometimes the exchange student's expectations of the United States or of the host family are quite unreasonable or inaccurate. A common complaint expressed by exchange students is that their U.S. "sister" or "brother" ignores them much of the time, going off with friends and leaving the foreign guest at home. Or the food, the bedroom, the shower, the television, the stereo, smoking, drinking, or clothing might be the problem. The host family may feel that the exchange student is a spoiled brat, very self-centered, and in general cold.

How will you get involved in all these problems? You must serve as the counselor, advocate, and wailing wall for all who fall under your charge. Exchange students are expected to know enough English to be able to function in the mainstream classrooms, but they are sometimes assigned to an ESL class for additional instruction in the intricacies of the English language. When students are unhappy, they perform poorly, if at all, in class. You have a choice: to try to deal with the issue with a view toward getting learning back on track, or to pretend nothing is wrong and hope the problem will go away. After experimenting with, and failing in, the latter approach a few times, you will probably opt for clearing the air, come what may. Occasionally, specifically planned lessons on cultural differences will suffice. More often, however, you will need to intervene in an effort to reestablish communication between the exchange student and the host family.

Foreign professional families assigned to do a tour of duty in the United States occasionally place their children in U.S. public schools. These families typically take a great deal of interest in the academic progress of their children and often demand that teachers, including you, be strict in enforcing academic requirements. This rigidity often contrasts sharply with what the visiting foreign students know to be the work load of their U.S.-born peers, resulting in conflicts between parent and child, between student and teacher, and perhaps between parent and teacher, depending on the perspective of the latter.

The home and community experiences of language minority students vary as much as those of their U.S.-born peers. These experiences affect the classroom performance of both language minority and native English-speaking students, but you will most likely get more involved with the out-of-class activities of your students than the mainstream teacher does. This involvement will derive from the demands your students will place on you for social support services, but your own concern for the welfare of your charges will also be an important factor.

For you, then, educating your students should mean teaching them academic skills as well as showing them how to cope as they adjust to life in an English-speaking society.

Note

1. A suicide hot-line service.

chapter four

The Student and the School

Sometimes we seem to have so much power to change these kids, but at other times we seem only able to sit back and watch things happen.
—Chris, 1990

FOCUSING QUESTIONS

★ When does the relationship between the ESL teacher and the language minority child begin?

★ What is the nature of this relationship?

★ How do mainstream teachers react to language minority children?

★ What cultural differences cause misinterpretations by mainstream teachers?

★ What kinds of relationships do language minority students have with their classmates?

★ What factors seem to affect these relationships?

★ How do English-speaking students feel about the cultures of language minority students?

★ What is the effect of placing language minority siblings in the same classroom?

★ Why is the ESL teacher so important to the development of the language minority students' English language skills?

★ What nonacademic needs does the ESL teacher typically address?

Most often the principal and secretary register all students, including those from language minority backgrounds. It will not be unusual, however, for them to involve you in the registration of your future students, especially when the principal is unaccustomed to dealing with children from non-English backgrounds. Whenever your first contact occurs, you immediately become the bridge between the student and the rest of the world.

The language minority student depends on you not only for instruction in English but for guidance and assistance in nearly every problematic situation, both in school and out. This forced dependency often creates a sort of love-hate relationship that affects both routine interaction and performance in learning activities. In the long run, however, most students come to value the selfless advocacy freely provided over the months and years. Hard-core misfits may return "just for a visit" to report on their activities since dropping out. And to the extent that they seem to be adjusting to life in the United States, you will experience a sense of accomplishment, a feeling that your contribution did make a difference after all.

Language minority students provoke a curious array of responses among mainstream teachers. Some teachers panic as soon as they learn that a linguistically different child has been assigned to their room. Others take a mother-hen stance and all but refuse to let colleagues intervene with "their" student.

Varied, too, are mainstream teachers' reactions to your suggestions. Sometimes they will claim that the youngster knows English perfectly ("I've heard him talking on the playground—he even swears!"); sometimes they will insist the child is mentally handicapped and needs to be evaluated. Some will be grateful for assistance with instruction, but some will attempt to consign only the most trivial of academic activities to you. In general, the younger (and cuter) the child, the more possessive the mainstream classroom teacher is. Contrariwise, if the child is older or somewhat of a behavior problem, the erstwhile mother hen will quickly tell you, "He's all yours!"

---★---

A readiness kid I have is in a flippant stage right now, and when I came to see her today, she was very flippant with me. A Cambodian boy who had been in private school but is now in fourth grade went through a period of that just this year with his teacher—he was very flippant with her, but she felt that he just didn't know any better. I believed that he knew better at one time but was going through another stage. The teacher also thought, and I agree with her, that he couldn't understand the linguistic subtleties of his classmates very well. They could get away with things that he couldn't because he couldn't finesse the verbal challenges to authority as they could. I was glad that she was sympathetic to this difference and that she was trying to bring him around.

---★---

One of my students was beginning to notice differences in register,[1] and his teacher announced that he was totally obstreperous and obnoxious. When I said, "No, he's learning," she replied, "Well, he can learn it somewhere else—I don't stand for this kind of behavior in my class."

In my opinion, being flippant is evidence of learning. The kids are imitating their peers but not getting it quite right.

Some of the older girls have terrible mouths. I tell them, "You cannot swear in English because you don't realize the force of the expressions." With the little kids I teach registers in a nonconfrontational way. With the older kids I don't do too much lecturing; they fall asleep. Instead I take up the problem on a case-by-case basis. I thought it might be good to practice register with role playing, but I found that this activity makes students vulnerable to personal attacks.

★

Not all behavior problems are linguistic in nature. As is true of English-speaking students, language minority students challenge authority in many ways.

★

A high school student was kicked out of school last week. Apparently, the last straw was not his smoking during school so much as his blowing smoke in the face of the teacher who caught him. It was the last in a long line of problems with

61
The Student and the School

authority. He came around to tell me about it, with that desperately I-don't-care look on his face. I haven't seen him since.

★

The degree to which language minority students interact with their English-speaking peers seems to depend on multiple factors: age, ethnic background, number of compatriots in the same school or area, and sex. In general, female Southeast Asian students, especially the older ones, seem to develop more friendships with U.S.-born students than do their male counterparts. Play and leisure activities for the males seem to be more confined to family and ethnic group. The males also begin to seek gainful employment as soon as they are able.

Within the school, relations with other students depend considerably on the attitude of the greater community toward the various ethnic groups. In smaller communities, such as those described in this text, the English-speaking majority usually welcomes the new arrivals either out of compassion for their refugee status or because they hope to broaden their cultural horizons through contact with representatives of other ethnic backgrounds.

★

Early September: I love the feeling of weaving individuals into a group. The beginning class developed "fellow feeling" almost immediately, but it has taken the advanced class longer, in part because we had to start off with so much testing. This week they've suddenly started giggling together and making jokes, usually in that order, and asking each other questions, all except my oldest boy, who is fading. Sometimes I look over at him sitting next to me and feel almost that he's becoming transparent. He spends most of the time with his head on the table, blocking out everyone, and speaks so softly that I can't hear him. The other boy in the group doesn't know how to handle him but does a kind of "Hail, fellow, well met!" number that the phantom responds to, faintly. The girls smile but don't know quite what to say. We do a lot of communication activities in which they speak to each other, and the disappearing one is sort of a sump into which their ideas sink.

In the advanced class a student shared with the others aloud and with me in his journal his sorrow at his grandfather's death. I was impressed at the way the other students sympathized. The students help each other in ways that teachers can never touch.

--- ★ ---

The English-speaking students generally demonstrate an initial curiosity about the various language minorities and welcome presentations by the different ethnic groups that depict one or more aspects of the foreign culture, particularly foreign holidays and celebrations. Some U.S.-born students like trying the exotic foods prepared by the ESL students or their family members, and even those who are too finicky to try the strange-looking dishes exhibit a genuine interest in finding out what the newcomers eat.

---★---

What a relief! They pulled it off! I wasn't sure how the fifth graders would respond to my kids. I think having the mother of one of the Cambodians there made a big difference. Usually my high school kids are so shy, but they really got into answering questions about Cambodia. I'm glad we handled it the way we did. If the classroom teachers hadn't done some preparatory activities, it wouldn't have gone so well. I wasn't sure whether I should make some introductory remarks or not, but I'm glad I did because it seemed to help to focus the discussion. The fifth graders were all ears when my kids were describing their experiences as refugees. I doubt they could really imagine what it was like, but the visuals helped, and, most of all, they seemed to pick up the emotional vibes. Anyway, I'm very pleased. All the time we spent practicing—writing about it and talking about it—paid off. I guess I'm just like a mother to those kids. I was worried about them falling on their faces, but now they're talking about doing it again!

---★---

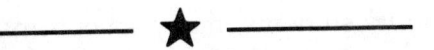

I can't believe it! I should have been prepared after our presentations to the fifth grade social studies group, but I guess I can't escape those "opening night" butterflies. Christmas in Mexico! I actually felt like I was there. It reminded me of the celebrations I saw when I was in Peace Corps training. What a great job they did with the *posadas*. The kids who played Mary and Joseph were absolutely fantastic. The singing and the special foods the parents brought were good. And the Mexican hot chocolate! Boy, was *that* a hit! The kids loved frothing it up with the *molinillo*. Frankly, I never thought they'd do it. Every other day the kid playing Joseph would tell me he was bowing out. Can you believe it? We'd already scheduled an assembly for the whole middle school, the high school drama club was building us a set and helping with costumes and props, and he wanted to quit. So did I, believe me, but the show must go on. The best part is that things happened that I didn't expect. Whether it was the audience or what, I don't know, but those kids really turned it on. It was beautiful. Would I do it again? Would I be in this position if I weren't a sucker for punishment?

---★---

Although an occasional problem will develop between an ESL student and an English-speaking peer, the most frequent conflicts are between siblings. Because of the small numbers of language minority students, many schools insist on grouping students by approximate grade levels or perhaps by level of proficiency. Such a requirement often results in the placement of two or more family members in the same instructional group, nearly always leading to a decrease in learning for one or more of the siblings.

The interaction between the family members varies, as does the response of each individual to the conflict, but the result is always the same: the focus of attention is on the conflict, not on the lesson at hand. Our experiences have convinced us that, if at all possible, siblings should always be separated for instructional purposes.

———★———

*R*esistance continues from the new Vietnamese boy. The poor kid is undoubtedly feeling all kinds of pressures to succeed, to be the head of his family, to look as though he isn't totally overwhelmed by the United States. He's reacting in what is, to me, a rather annoying way, and I gather it's bothering his sponsors, too.

First of all, he picks on his sister. She's reacting to all the stresses by going totally silent and trying to look invisible; when she says a word, he corrects it (her pronunciation is better than his). When she makes a mistake, he laughs, inviting me to share his mirth. When she is slow, he sighs loudly, picks up a book to look at, and lets me know that this is a waste of his time.

"You feel that the class is too easy for you?" He nodded. "What grammar do you want to learn?"

"Like tense." (He had to repeat this, because I couldn't understand.) "Presen' ten', futu' ten'."

I finally had had enough. I pulled a picture of a baby out of the picture file and held it up. "You are a man, but for English you are a baby. You cannot run. You must start at the beginning." He smiled. I've probably mortally insulted him.

I want to get him and his sister separated. Aside from the fact that he picks on her and she won't open up while he's in the room, their styles are different. She's not ready to talk; she needs a totally different kind of class than he does. He wants to be pushed—I suspect he wants whatever kind of harsh and punitive system he undoubtedly did well in before, preferably one in which he won't have to *speak* English but will write interminable translation exercises. I'd love to be able to take the time to help the girl feel comfortable enough to participate. I'd also like to help the boy relax and learn more efficiently.

─────── ★ ───────

One of the seniors is my joy this year. He writes in his journal every few days without prompting. He is going like gangbusters in the new vocational graphic arts course. He got his driver's license and passed the 3-minute speech competency in the same week. During finals, he wrote a competency paragraph that passed, making him a full-fledged senior who needs only passing grades to graduate. But he's not slacking off. He's reading *Scholastic Scope*[2] and writing about it, and is enthusiastic about doing some math for graphic arts. Most interesting is what precipitated this turnaround: the departure of his sister. He has had to be grouped with her for ESL, social studies, science, and some other courses for the 5 years he's been here (and in the United States). He has always been content to let her attract all the attention and would try to be invisible in any class she was in, even though he usually understood more than she. He let teachers think he didn't understand rather than communicate. He let us know from time to time that he didn't think much of her intelligence and behavior, but he didn't change. As soon as she was gone, I began to hear a different story from his teachers as well as see it myself. I guess it's just a reminder of how truly important the personality factor is.

---⭐---

We don't have enough students always to allow for the separation of brothers and sisters, but there are things we could probably do when we suspect a problem. Absurd as it may seem, even though siblings are taking the same course or using the same ESL text, we may have to individualize, dividing up the class time. I've become convinced that a smaller dose of one-on-one time is just as valuable as or more valuable than a larger dose of group time—especially if the student has a negative attitude for some reason. If the students are out in the mainstream, working in a group most of the day, something that is theirs alone is valuable.

★

Language minority students spend much of the school day in an English-language environment and acquire bits and pieces of the English language automatically whenever what they hear or read is comprehensible. Thus the language minority student is not dependent solely on you for training in English language skills. Without a doubt, however, the language minority student's most important relationship within the school community will be with you.

★

My high school ESL students seem very demanding. They want words spelled, concepts explained. They ask all the questions they're too shy or inhibited to ask in their other classes: "Why does the library need to know where I live?" "What is a sonnet?" "What's the difference between a quiz and a test in Algebra?" "What's wrong with saying 'ain't' anyhow?"

They want reassurance. They want their wit appreciated and their beliefs validated.

It suddenly strikes me: so many of the mainstream teachers tell me things like, "He's so quiet that I hardly know he's in class." Perhaps the students feel the same. Do they fade out in their own eyes? As they hide behind their books, do they feel themselves lose substance? Perhaps the ESL class, with everything else it does, is the one place where the students can be sure that they really do exist by being demanding and having their demands met.

─────────★─────────

Language minority students will depend on you for many of their nonacademic needs as well. You will serve as advocate both in school and out; you will serve as cultural interpreter when members of the community do not understand foreign folkways; you will function as a parent, making sure your students are properly dressed for the weather conditions, checking on lunch supplies, and often providing lunch money from your personal funds so your students will not go hungry; you will listen patiently and counsel cautiously whenever your students come to you with tales of love affairs, real or imagined; of personal tragedies past or present; of the need to get visas or other legal documents; of values conflicts with parents or other family members; of physical, psychological or sexual abuse. You will have to perform some of the functions of the school nurse: monitoring the personal hygiene of your students, guiding them in sickness and accident prevention, and dealing with questions about sex that may have gone unasked in the sex education class.

---   ★   ---

Why is it that things that seem so trivial to us can really bend other people out of shape? One of my junior high kids came in today, and was he ever upset! He hadn't done an assignment for his social studies teacher, and the teacher told him he was consequently in the doghouse. "I'm not a dog! He called me a dog!" There was no chance I was going to start a lesson until he was calmed down. I explained, as best I could, where the expression came from and what it meant. He didn't seem totally convinced that he hadn't been pierced to the quick of his ego, but I patiently assured him that no one thought he was a dog. I must say, though, that if I ever have to smooth his feathers again, an avian metaphor may occur to me.

---   ★   ---

A student I've had off and on has another personality type. Off and on? Yes, because he has to be "on" in order to make anything work. When he decides he needs or wants ESL, he learns a lot. Otherwise, forget it. This year, for example, when he finally digested the fact that he would have to take the TOEFL, he was willing to work hard on preparing for it. Until then I felt as though I was talking to a wall. One of the other keys to his personality is what I call a fear of ghettoization. He runs from ESL, from colleges with great ESL programs or bilingual-bicultural programs, because there are too many foreign students or too many Cambodians. He doesn't want to be stereotyped. This kind of personality must perceive ESL as necessary and useful, not as punishment. Earlier mainstreaming, supportive teachers, and no hard-and-fast rules about levels or exit points mean that the necessity and usefulness of ESL are not always clear. ESL teachers have to keep a student like that in their orbit and keep offering support, I guess.

---★---

How do you explain to third graders about personal tragedies? Ever since that apartment house burned down last week, killing two kids from one of my schools, I haven't been able to get the children to drop the subject. I guess it's because the school made such a big deal about it with announcements and assemblies and counseling and so forth. My kids didn't really understand, but they wanted to be part of the action.

I didn't think I could handle it on any kind of a philosophical level—like, "Why do bad things happen to good people?"—so I decided to do a lesson or two on fires and fire safety. It turned out very nicely, and I think I even persuaded the students to go home and talk to their parents about some of the safety tips we discussed. I worry especially about the families from Southeast Asia who mind the cold so much. They might attempt to use unsafe heating methods in the winter.

I thought the lesson went so well I decided to try it with my high school group. Unfortunately, they didn't seem to share the concern of the younger kids. In fact, several bragged about smoking in bed. At that point, I gave up and went on to another activity. Were they just putting me on? I hope so.

---------★---------

If you don't draw the line, you will often be called on to assist the student not only during school hours but 24 hours a day, including weekends. You will not be able to stop thinking about the concerns of your students when the day ends, nor when the week or even the school year ends. The sense of responsibility is continuous, but you must be vigilant to maintain some balance in your life. You have to be able to say "no" firmly and definitively when appropriate.

The demand for parentlike concern and guardianship will often create an emotional bond between you and your students. You will become vulnerable to unkind or insensitive behavior on the part of your students.

---⭐---

Is there some basic need for protection that I am not meeting? I guess most ESL teachers, myself included, take on a sort of motherly role vis-à-vis our students. But lately I've noticed that my high school females seem to be trying to find other teachers to attach themselves to. At first, I felt somewhat hurt. "Why do they need someone else?" I asked myself. After thinking about it, I realized that even though I feel very close to them and they share their most intimate feelings with me in their journals, they probably feel a need to distance themselves from me—their *in loco parentis*—just to gain a measure of independence.

The guys, on the other hand, don't seem to have connections with anyone. Most of them work after school and don't have time to hang around for small talk.

---⭐---

And of course you are a teacher as well as a parent figure: of language, culture, interpersonal relations, mathematics, science, social studies, art, and music.

---⭐---

Although they are often critical of the U.S. educational system, the exchange students seem terribly normal in comparison with some of my charges. Today they were studying for a test on adverbs and adjectives in their "real" English class. They asked me to explain, and for a few minutes I had the refreshing experience of teaching a nice, simple grammar class. One student really liked the neat rule on when to use *more* and *most* as opposed to *-er* and *-est*. Another insisted that her English teacher said that a sentence like "Detroit is largest city in Michigan" was correct. We argued about it, with the first student saying at intervals in baritone counterpoint, "Second largest, Detroit is second largest."

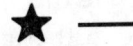

★

At the end of class, I apologized to the students because it appears that they won't get a grade for ESL. They shrugged it off, and one who has sat and glowered through the classes said, "I don't care about grade. I learn more English in this class than in any other one." After they left, I just sat and glowed for a few minutes.

★

It's tough enough to teach without having the students tell me how to do it. Give me a break! When the new

Vietnamese boy came in, he knew how to learn English: You learn English by memorizing the 12 sentence types and the rules for making each one of them, looking up the words in your bilingual dictionary, and applying the rules and the words to each other! Unfortunately the sentences he came out with were totally incomprehensible. He was very angry that I did not give him grammar-translation exercises, and the first 2 weeks of classes consisted of a power struggle between him and me as to how the class was to be run. We hit rock bottom the day I said, "OK, open your book," and he looked at me totally blankly. I picked it up and said, "What's this?" expecting to hear, "It's a *book*," but he said, "Notebook," and I said, "It's a *book*." "Notebook." Say, "It's a *book*." "Notebook." I held up a notebook, and I held up a book, and we went through the whole thing. He did not know how to say, "It's a book." He did not believe in the use of the copula. So we went through a bunch of sentence pattern drills, and at the end he looked at me and said, "Teacher, too easy." Language learning has to be tough, something that makes you *squirm*. Look, I have nothing against grammar. Some of my best friends are grammarians. But I think you have to find the *teachable moment*. That's why when my students write, I always talk about their errors—not at first, but before we drop the piece. I point things out and see how they respond, and if it looks like they're going to grasp the concept, I'll expand on it. It works.

The weight of previous experience is hard to deal with in some students. They have picked up attitudes and bad habits that slow them down in my view. After a while, my student began to look at me as if maybe I knew what I was doing. In fact, the other day he gave me a great compliment—he said I should go and teach in the refugee camps in the Philippines. At least I think it was a compliment. . . .

---★---

Parent, counselor, nurse, friend, confessor, and teacher—these are the roles you play as you help your students adjust to life at school and in the United States.

Notes

1. Linguists use the term *register* to describe the level of formality in language use. In speech there are five registers ranging from intimate comments to oratory.
2. *Scholastic Scope* is a magazine of literary readings selected for English classes available from Scholastic, Inc., 730 Broadway, New York, NY 10003-9538. Scholastic, Inc., also publishes other magazines of interest to ESL teachers.

chapter five

Families

FOCUSING QUESTIONS

★ Why must ESL teachers have frequent contact with the parents of their students?

★ Why are parent handbooks useful?

★ What special problems arise with notes sent home from school?

★ Why are parent-teacher conferences important for language minority families?

★ How can the ESL teacher use parents to enhance a multicultural curriculum?

★ In what ways do ESL teachers often assist parents with their needs in the community?

★ Why might conflicts develop between parents and the ESL teacher?

Unquestionably, you will have more direct personal contact with the families of your students than any other teacher in the school system does. In many instances this interaction involves issues relating to the students, but you will probably spend considerable time and energy dealing with the needs of the adult immigrants themselves.

As indicated in chapter 4, you will often participate in the registration process. Otherwise, your first contact with a student's family will generally consist of an attempt to communicate what ESL is. You might make home visits to determine the level of English proficiency of the family, enabling you to send appropriate notices home.

---★---

I went over to the home of the family of the new Vietnamese children. The father still looks shell-shocked. I went through my spiel about the schools, using all my best generic Southeast Asian body language. They didn't seem terribly impressed, but they didn't laugh at me or kick me out.

---★---

*P*hone call, interrupting work with the second graders:
"This is Mrs. Lee. I have daughter, 5 year old. She can go kindergarten? She no English."
"Oh, yes, we have a good kindergarten, and we will help her learn English. What is your daughter's name?"
"Groria."
We all spent several days waiting for "Groria" to join the kindergarten, but she never turned up. I'm afraid it was my fault for not switching gears from teaching to administering fast enough.

---- ★ ----

*I*t's tough dealing with children of illiterate parents who don't realize the importance of having books around the house. But yesterday, when I was doing a home visit, I saw the father sitting with his youngest son, who was trying to read a book. The father knew enough English to correct a couple of the words—it would have made a beautiful picture.

I asked the father what he noticed about the way his son was learning to read. He answered, "Well, they bring home these books." "Yes," I said, "they don't do words beginning with 'A' one week, 'B' the next, 'C' the week after, and so on." "Yes," he said, "my son points to the words, and he reads them." I asked, "Does he always say the word that he's pointing to?" And the father said, "No, I've noticed that he doesn't always say the right word. But he knows the story very well." I replied, "But you can see that he's reading more and more of them and he enjoys reading to you."

It's so nice for the parents when they do understand something—they feel so much better.

---- ★ ----

We have found it useful to distribute a parent handbook such as the one in Appendix A. Written in basic English, the handbook answers the questions most parents have and provides practical information they can use in their responses to requests by the teacher and child. If the parents are involved

Chapter 5

in English language study themselves, the handbook can serve as a practical text for learning activities of all types. Delivering the handbook personally will ensure that it reaches the parents' hands and will enable you to instruct parents in its use.

---★---

Just had a phone call from a parent who complained that my handbook is too long and too complicated. And I thought it was so great! Maybe they can't read it or didn't want to, or maybe I just didn't make myself clear. Maybe basic English is basic only if you already know English. Anyway, hardly a day goes by when I don't have to deal with some cross-cultural issue. My kids are good when they want to be, but they learn very quickly that they can manipulate their parents by misleading them. Then the parents discover the deceit and subsequently won't believe anything. I have my work cut out for me.

For example, a third grade teacher told me the other day that she was concerned about the appearance of one of my kids. He comes to school unbathed and often wears ripped pants that make it obvious he's not wearing undershorts. She wanted *me* to do something about it. I dutifully trotted over to the kid's house after school. I could tell that his mother really didn't want to talk to me by the way she hung back and didn't invite me in or anything. I explained the situation to an older sister who had to serve as interpreter. I probably was a little tough on them, but they had to understand that if they want to send their children to our schools, they must learn to compromise. They can dress as they like on the weekends!

---★---

The matter of sending notes home, problematic even with U.S.-born students, will require a good deal of reflection on your part. You must ask yourself or the classroom teacher, "Is this something these parents need to know?" If the reply is negative, you will most likely discard the note. If the information is essential, the challenge then becomes how to make sure that the information finds its way home, is read, and is understood. Again, you will probably make a trip to the home or perhaps ask one member of each ethnic group to help you prepare a translation for distribution.

---★---

I called a student's mother today to remind her that her daughter shouldn't go to kindergarten this afternoon. She said she knew that; they'd gotten the note after all. Another victory! Both she and her husband had read the note on their own and done what was appropriate. In fact, both of them took it as a matter of course. (Then they tell me that they feel they'll never learn enough English to get along. They don't realize what tremendous strides they've made.) She also said that her daughter's birthday is the 10th. She pointed out that in Vietnam they celebrate only the 1st and 60th birthdays but that her daughter told her that, because they're in the United States now, she thinks they ought to celebrate birthdays U.S. style.

───── ★ ─────

It is particularly difficult when mainstream teachers request money or food items for a party. For example, each year the students have the option of signing up for a sort of "book-of-the-month" club with the payment of a nominal fee.

───── ★ ─────

After school I went around to see the parents about the book subscriptions. I don't let the kids sign up themselves because they just buy junk. I go directly to the parents and explain that they should give me $5 to buy good books for their kids, and most of them do. I feel I'm giving the parents the kind of control they would have if they had control of English. The money will probably run out, but I usually keep buying the books anyway. The kids really like them.

―――― ★ ――――

*E*ven the parents who have been through schools in their own countries are so confused by what happens in U.S. schools that they have a terrible time when the notes come home and the kid says, "I've got to have $5 for tomorrow." The parents have to decide if they really *do* need $5 for tomorrow, if they have to sign the slip, why they have to sign the permission form, or what it means to bring "eight paper cups and eight paper napkins." When asked to provide these for a Halloween party, the mother of one of my students wondered, "Can't I send all the paper cups in? I have to buy paper cups especially for this, and I only send in eight? What do I do with the other ones?"

Much of what I have to do consists of filtering all the printed matter that gets sent home to the parents. A lot of parents think the kids are conning them all the time—and they're right! One of my students wanted to be a witch for the Halloween party, but, she told me, "My mother has no money; I don't have costume." I said, "We can work out the costume," and she said, "Oh, no, my mother won't spend money for a costume." So I went over to her house, and I told her mother, "Your daughter wants to be a witch for Halloween," and she said, "Yes, I know witch." I asked, "Do you have a black dress?" The girl said, "No, she doesn't!" but the mother said, "I do too!" I told the mother, "Let your daughter wear the black dress. She'll take good care of it, and she can be a witch—you don't have to buy a costume." The girl gave me the dirtiest look!

---   ★   ---

You should try hard to convince the parents to come to conferences and parents' night open houses. It is not easy. Among the many reasons why parents don't visit their children's school more often are embarrassment over poor English language skills, a culturally based awe of teachers and the educational establishment, fatigue after a hard day's work, lack of baby-sitters for the children, lack of transportation, and misunderstanding of the reason they are being asked to come to the school. Some, for example, believe it is because their child is performing poorly or behaving badly.

---   ★   ---

We had an open house tonight. I wish I could think of some way to get more of my kids' parents to come. We're concerned all the time that our kids' parents don't have the skills for interacting with the school or don't care to do so. I know how they feel—inadequate in so many ways—but I wish I could communicate to them that I would be as accepting of them as I am of their children. I'm not the reason they don't come, and I know that. They always welcome me when I visit their homes, as I often must.

Almost every Cambodian parent did come; in fact, the Cambodians stood out as shining lights because overall attendance wasn't that great. I know they had a lot of anxiety about coming—so good for them!

One problem is that we don't structure the program right, even for the native English-speaking parents. We run the parents through a sample schedule using language that is no doubt unfathomable, give them a teacher's overview of what happens in the class, and that's it. There's very little opportunity for interaction with the teacher.

It is important for parents to come anyway. I can't be as effective as I should be without their involvement. When they visit the schools, they can see samples of their children's work, get a feeling for the classroom environment, and become aware of facilities like the gym. Then when the kid comes home and makes some comment about what went on in school, the parents can join in a meaningful discussion.

★

Sometimes parents do come. Often they will ask you to accompany them to parent-teacher conferences to serve as interpreter (whether or not you speak their language) and cultural go-between. And very often the mainstream teacher will ask you to be present. Even when you remain totally silent, as you sometimes may, you will make all parties feel comfortable. It is very useful for parents to tour the physical facilities because subsequent activity reports by their children will make more sense. Some parents have had little or no formal schooling, but even those who are well educated have generally studied in very different learning environments.

---★---

I think conferences with classroom teachers help too. I know it makes the parents of my students anxious to sit down face to face with a teacher, so I usually sit in and act as a go-between. That gives them the confidence they need. The best luck I've had is getting the parents to come to more informal events or plays in the evening. The parents feel less threatened, yet they have a chance to see what's going on and even an opportunity to interact a little bit with some of the English-speaking parents. Whenever something special is coming up, I always make an effort to persuade the parents to attend.

When we don't have good parental support, things go downhill. One kid's family tries everything to remain uninvolved with school. Every time we suggest a parent-teacher conference, they resist and offer countless excuses. They won't listen to me when I tell them that homework is more important than forcing the kid to watch the baby. There is absolutely no support for this child, and, sadly, the school results reflect that. I'm going to try to arrange a meeting with the family at the sponsor's house. Maybe we can come to a meeting of the minds in neutral territory.

It's very hard for kids when they are getting mixed messages from home and school. Another little boy who is a holy terror at home—they can't control him at all—is in a class where the teacher believes in a touchy-feely kind of permissive approach to group dynamics. The parents feel he should be beaten and kept after school and stuff. I ask myself, "What is this doing to the kid? How can he interpret both messages and determine which applies where and when?" That's another reason I spend so much of my time trying to get the parents into the school: so that there is a chance the messages won't be mixed.

With the older kids, I've found that lack of parental involvement leads to all sorts of abuses of school policies, especially attendance policies. The kids will write their own excuse notes, and the parents seem unaware of what's going on. But I can't get uptight about it; I have other concerns that deserve my energy.

---★---

I think the hardest thing I have to do is to explain to someone the details of a student's progress, which teachers, administrators, parents, and the kids themselves ask me to do continually. Straight talk doesn't seem to work, so I use a bunch of tricks. For instance, I tell my students that "learning a language is like trying to cross a river by stepping on the stones. The stones are the bits you understand, but there is a lot still under the water. The more you understand, the more the stones will look like a bridge." I'm not sure they believe me.

Today the host parents of an exchange student came in. He's been here only 3 months, but they're concerned that he's not learning enough English. "But he can even tell jokes," I responded. "For example, the other day he told me if I ate too much chicken, I would get chicken pox!" They weren't assuaged. I talked to his classroom teacher, who, it turns out, is upset because the host parents are upset. It seems that the kid is feeling homesick and depressed primarily because a holiday, important to him in his homeland, passed unnoticed in the United States. I tried to persuade the parents to be understanding, advising them that little new learning could take place until the affective filter[1]—those unhappy emotions—had been dealt with.

★

Many parents will gladly come in to do cultural demonstrations of one sort or another. Topics might include costumes, dance, music, arts and crafts, cooking, and holiday celebrations. If the presenters are good role models (you should screen them before you tender an invitation), they not only enhance the status of their child and other members of the ethnic group but also contribute to a lessening of ethnocentricity in the school community.

---★---

*A*lways something new in this job! One morning, a student who is moving away from ESL came in at 7:30 and said, "My mother's here. She wants to see you." Apparently, she had started an evening job and wanted to know if she could come to school. She had always loved school. When she was a little girl, she begged to study with the monks, who finally convinced her father that she ought to be able to and not have to care for her little brother. Her mother was ill at the time.

Living now in the United States, she wanted to improve her English to increase her job security. I said, "Sure," and she started coming every day. What a joy! Her son is one of my best students, but he won't come near me when she's around. The other kids really seem to respect her. She's a great help with the discussions—she is articulate, and she can validate the historical and cultural comments made in class. She's started writing an autobiography. It's pretty exciting stuff to read, but it's even more exciting to see her start to bloom academically. I hope she can continue her studies. She's already told me that it's tough keeping the kids under control while she works at night. Maybe we need night care as well as day care!

---★---

As indicated, contact with your students' families is not limited to the school grounds or to academic matters. Just as you will immediately become the ombudsman for the language minority children, you will soon slip into this role for their families as well. Whatever their problems—utilities, landlords, driving licenses, police, the courts, misunderstandings with sponsoring groups—you will be asked to deal with them. This multifaceted advocacy means that you will become intimately knowledgeable about the parents of your current students and about the intrigues of the entire immigrant community. You will be privy to all the gossip and the scandals as well as the good news. You will often be invited to take part in celebrations much as if you were a member of the in-group, because for the most part family members will recognize and appreciate your considerable efforts on their behalf.

---   ★   ---

Notes from the social services department: Called the dentist for a student's family; his mom doesn't understand the bill. Called the junior high about an ex-student who is behaving badly, skipping school, etc. His mother is terribly upset. Called Family Services (this took several calls) to see if the woman who has dealt with Southeast Asians could arrange to meet with the upset mother. Called School Lunch to make sure things are OK for another student's family. In my spare time I taught English.

Later: The boy's mom worked out how she was going to pay the dentist bill. I think my upset mother is going to meet with the counselor. School Lunch seems to be satisfied with the latest forms.

---★---

I went over to visit a woman who had just been the victim of domestic violence. She was carrying on in a big way and wanted to tell me all about it. I asked her if she wanted me to find someone to look after her kids while we talked, but she said, "Oh, no, they're all right." And she proceeded to let me in on all the gory details while the kids played at her bedside.

---★---

A runner came up to my classroom with a note saying that Jacinto was on the phone again. (He's the Panamanian who wants to bring his sister to the United States. I think he sees ESL at the high school as a way for her to get a visa. That's fine with me; I'm all in favor of people being allowed to travel.) I told him that ESL was available and that, because his sister is 17 years old, she could certainly attend high school if she came here. Jacinto said he had called to find out how to get a student visa. I told him I would check on it and then went down to the office to talk about him.

The secretary told me how fascinating all of this was. She hadn't expected to have to deal with foreign students and wondered what this "Colón" was that I kept talking about. I told her that, as I understood it, the sister would have to apply for a student visa at the U.S. consulate in Colón and that the high school could probably send a letter saying that she was going to be a student, but that it should be made clear to Jacinto that she would have to plan on taking a full course load to qualify as a student. I suggested that the secretary talk to the local refugee coordinator about this. If anyone knows the rules, she's the one.

We agreed that after she talks with the refugee coordinator, she will take the matter up with Curriculum to make sure that everything's OK with the school before she calls Jacinto back. The secretary is new here, and I was overwhelmed that she offered to do all of this phoning. I don't think anyone else has made such an offer; she kept saying how interesting it all was!

───────── ★ ─────────

For this evening, phone calls to José to set up a lesson and to Maria to see how she and her son are doing in their new home.

───────── ★ ─────────

Not all your efforts will be appreciated. At times you will not be able to approve conscientiously of what is going on in a given ethnic community, and at times you must, or will choose to, come between the parents and one or more of your students. The matter of clothing is a case in point. Some immigrant families seem not to understand the impact of the northern winter. Although they themselves complain frequently of the cold, they may send their children to school dressed for mid-July when it is windy and 20 degrees below zero. Although the families typically react negatively to intervention on this score, you will probably feel obliged to protect the interests of the child.

A similar issue is the style and condition of clothing. Although you might be comfortable with sartorial diversity, you should not tolerate clothing that exposes the student to ridicule or harm. Again, you will risk incurring the wrath of the parents by advising them that while their children are at school, they must respect certain standards of attire. At the same time, you should be careful to point out that when the children are at home, the parents are free to dress them as they choose.

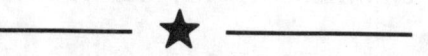

─────────── ★ ───────────

I had to visit a student's home today. A third grader has been coming to school in shirttails, and my God, it must be 20 below zero first thing in the morning. You'd think it would be a matter of common sense, wouldn't you? Well, so much for common sense. I knew the sponsoring family was very concerned and doting, so I couldn't believe they had neglected to provide winter clothing. Nonetheless, it might have been an oversight.

"Tell me," I inquired, "does Chanta have a winter coat?" "Oh, yes," came the swift reply, "but he won't wear it." Soon after my interlocutor had provided this explanation, another family member appeared at the door displaying a beautiful and warm ski parka. No sign of any wear. "But don't you realize that Chanta could get very sick by being exposed to such cold?" I naively asked. "But he won't wear it," came the incomprehensible reply.

There are six adults in the household. This morning Bo told me that the kid's mom had been very upset at my interference. "But you don't understand," he said. "There is nothing they can do if the kid won't wear his jacket." He's right. I don't understand how the six adults in that household can't persuade an 8-year-old child to do something that is so clearly good for him and comfortable as well.

There is some weird sort of family power game going on, and I don't want to be sucked in. (Not much chance of that—I don't think I'm ever going to be invited back.)

———★———

Another home visit today. One of the reasons I made this visit was that the classroom teacher was concerned about a few things. I had thought that most of them were under control because the parents had come in, the little girl was getting her lunch money in (a problem at first), was taking notices home, and after a few misses was bringing back papers to be signed—permission slips and so on. This girl caused real headaches when she didn't have a permission slip the day her class went to the apple orchard and her father had to be called at work.

The teacher was still concerned that the girl was not properly dressed to go out at recess—and our school policy is that everyone goes out! Teachers get very upset when they see kids without jackets or mittens or hats, and the fact of the matter is that a lot of refugee children do seem to wear fewer clothes, especially the young ones. It's amazing how they go around with so little on. The teacher was concerned that this girl dress better for school—that she wear socks and so on.

I knew that the parents left for work at 7:00 in the morning and the child left for school at 8:15 or 8:20. I found out that her brother was responsible for getting her dressed. When I visited the house I wanted to suggest that her mother and father lay out her clothes the night before, but I thought it was just a little bit too presumptuous, that these people had been in the United States too long for me to be telling them how things are done here. I brought up the topic and put the onus on the boy, who was basically responsible for it anyway. I spoke to him carefully and clearly so the parents could hear. I said, "Now, Kim Lee, before you let your sister out of the door, you *check*. Does she have warm socks on? Does she have her jacket? Does she have mittens? Does she have a hat? These are really important things, and you can check for these things."

I have found sometimes that, when these things come up, I have more success by indirectly querying all the child's siblings before going to the parents.

A young female student looked very dirty one week. Her hair was a mess, and I thought, "Gosh, nobody is seeing to it that she has a bath. But her parents are home at night. . . ." I didn't know what to think, so I asked her older sister—and I didn't say, "Your sister's hair is really dirty." I said, "Your sister is so cute! Her hair looks different this week. Did you put some gel on it or something? Are you guys trying to do something with her hair?" The girl answered, "Well, no. She did have a permanent a while back." I said, "Well, I don't know, her hair looked kind of sticky." She answered, "Gee, I don't even see my sister because she's in bed when I come home from work."

Then I knew that the two older kids didn't have any responsibility, only the younger brother. The parents, in my opinion, should do more. But at least becoming aware of the situation gave me some room for maneuvering: I now have a better idea of how the girl is cared for. I think I've become fairly masterful at eliciting information from my student's siblings without appearing to suggest that there's any problem, so I don't jump to conclusions and I don't take the wrong tack.

I've been told by more than one person that in this family the mother is just about holding together. I know she's not washing the kids' clothes enough, ironing, or doing other things as well as she might, but I can't change that.

Nonetheless, I still want to convey the teacher's concern—you have to see what you can do.

---   ★   ---

Perhaps the most serious breaches between you and the immigrant families will result from conflicts in cross-cultural values. Although these conflicts occasionally may take the form of your providing moral support for a teenage girl whose parents are determined to go through with an arranged marriage she opposes, most often they will result from your encouraging the children to reach for their full potential in line with U.S. values. Many immigrant parents, especially Southeast Asians, believe that their sons should begin to work as soon as possible and that their daughters should marry and start families at the first opportunity. When you see the potential of many language minority students, it will be difficult for you to sit back in silence and let the parents' will be done—so difficult, in fact, that very often you will find occasions to present options to the students that they never knew existed and that, if chosen, would put their lives on a completely different course from the one projected by their families. There is no conflict over the goal; both you and the parents will want the best for the students. The conflict arises over differing interpretations of what is best as well as differing perceptions of the most appropriate means to achieve the goals. The challenge for you, then, is to help the students realize their dreams without antagonizing everyone in the process.

---★---

I recently learned that one of my Cambodian girls is suffering badly. Her family has arranged for her to marry a man nearly twice her age. She was aware of this cultural pattern, but, sadly for her, she had her eyes on another, much younger and more attractive man. She's pouring out all her feelings in the journal. She wants my advice, and she'd like me to intervene with the family. I really feel for her, but what are the limits of my responsibilities? What right do I have to interfere with the family's plans? Am I my sister's keeper?

---★---

If you agree to intervene, perhaps you will justify your intervention by perceiving the parents as sometimes uninformed and narrow in perspective. Or perhaps the more intimate contact you will have with the students means that you will develop a higher loyalty to them and will feel constrained to protect them from what you view as unreasonable demands.

---- ★ ----

Who was it that said, "There's no growth without pain"? I've been agonizing over a girl who was eliciting my support in fighting her parents' plans to marry her off. Over the summer she did a 180-degree turn and came back to school engaged. For maybe a day or two I thought, "Was I really a fool? Was I really wrong?" Then I began to see that I wasn't wrong. She'd done it all out of fear and cowardice and perhaps to some degree to try to please her parents. When she told me today that she had made another 180-degree turn back, I was much more prepared and took everything with much more equanimity. In short, I really maintained my balance. In spite of the pain, I have learned a lot from this experience.

---- ★ ----

Every generation of immigrants makes its accommodations with the host country's values and ways of doing things. Most people agree that education is very important in this country. If a rice farmer's son goes to college and betters his situation while still managing to respect native cultural values, most families accept and even welcome it. All cultures have doctors, teachers, businessmen, and other professionals, but occupation is more class-related in other countries than it is here, a fact that may inhibit the aspirations of some immigrants.

Most women, U.S.-born or immigrant, have to work. It will probably be very difficult for you to accept cross-cultural notions of female subservience or inferiority. In addition to wanting to see your female students fulfilled, you may foresee that the families will ultimately understand education's contribution to earning power. The families of many immigrant students dream of having sufficient economic resources so that the younger females do not have to work even though the women of the older generations do. But you will most likely feel certain that the girls will have to work, and you will therefore probably believe that they should aspire to good jobs. Furthermore, given the cultural upheaval that immigration brings about, you will be aware that divorce is always a possibility. Thus you will most likely want to see your female students (as well as your males) be trained to be self-sufficient.

In your job as an ESL teacher, you will encounter situations where you must choose sides. And you will always be tempted to represent the interests of your students.

Note

1. *Affective filter* is a term used by language acquisition theorist Stephen Krashen (Krashen & Terrell, 1983) to denote the emotional obstacles to learning.

chapter six

Teachers in the Mainstream

FOCUSING QUESTIONS

★ What are the relationships between ESL and mainstream teachers like?

★ What factors lead to conflict or cooperation?

★ What is the role of the ESL teacher in dealing with ethnocentricity?

★ How do philosophical differences among mainstream teachers affect the ESL program?

★ What compromises must the ESL teacher make?

★ How can the ESL teacher bring about an appreciation of cultural diversity?

Relationships between you and the so-called mainstream teachers need time to evolve. Upon your arrival on the scene, or upon the establishment of a special program for language minority students, the other teachers nearly always have little if any understanding of your intended functions. At staff meetings they may display this naiveté by posing a series of ingenuous questions: "Do you really speak all those languages? You don't? Then how can you teach them English?"

"Isn't it wonderful the way children pick up languages?" Oomph! Every time I hear someone say that, my stomach muscles get as tight as a drumhead.

★

Because it is poorly understood, the ESL program, at least for some mainstream teachers, becomes the dumping ground for problem cases. The pressure is very strong to accommodate the wishes of the mainstream teachers, and you as a beginner may not have the self-confidence necessary to hold the line. In these cases, you will inevitably be asked to deal with all kinds of language remediation, not only for second language learners but for native speakers of English as well. Nonetheless, you should resist the temptation to be a remedial instructor for two important reasons: first, you probably will not have been trained as a remedial native language instructor and therefore might not use your and the student's time effectively and, second, to be seen or to see yourself solely as a remedial instructor would detract from your professional image.

★

Let's see. How many weeks are we into the school year? In any case, considerable time has elapsed, but finally the classroom teachers I work with seem to have decided where

ESL fits and what I have to offer them. I get more and more requests for cooperation, which I take to mean that they are beginning to respect the ESL function.

Nonetheless, there are still problems of communication. With some kids at the elementary level I'm basically doing social work. Don't mistake me, it has real value, and I think I do it well, but I do have an identity crisis at times. For example, I spend a lot of time reporting to teachers on how problems in the kid's family could be affecting behavior in class.

It still irks me a little when mainstream teachers see my role only as that of a remedial instructor. I don't believe I have enough time and continuity to develop the students to their full potential, but I can't convince myself that I'm doing any good if I just go in and drill. What we need is a cooperative approach. If I can get the mainstream teachers to work with me in dealing with the special needs of our language minority students, we could take a team approach to the education of these kids.

★

It was a relief to go over to the elementary school for a relatively simple afternoon. I was missing a few students (no kindergartners because of parent-teacher conferences, no third grader because of Art, no fifth grader because he's sick). I spent all my free time writing up a description of Rodrigo's English for his present teacher. He "graduated" from the ESL program at the end of last year, but I had to explain to his teacher that he still isn't where he'd be if he were a native speaker and that some skills will still need more work in class. Anyhow, his father wanted him to graduate from ESL as soon as possible.

───────★───────

Initially, you may encounter ethnocentricity on the part of some mainstream teachers. Their cultural insensitivity may result in offensive remarks or behaviors. You will need to invest considerable energy in educating these colleagues as well as in defending the students whose feelings are subject to abuse. Generally, after repeated discussions (one-on-one is the most effective way) and multicultural presentations attended by the entire school community (not necessarily at the same time), the mainstream teachers who hold ethnocentric views will come to realize that the language minority students have a tough advocate in you and that they, the mainstream teachers, must behave in culturally appropriate ways or they will be challenged.

With time, the mainstream teachers will come to understand your role and to appreciate your contribution to the school program. They will come to value rather than distrust ethnic diversity and will enthusiastically incorporate multicultural units, in which the ESL students participate, into their classroom programs.

---★---

After school there was an elementary school staff meeting, which I don't really need to attend but do for PR reasons. Besides, the meetings help me to keep up to date on what's happening with the mainstream curriculum. I've worked hard this year to get to know the classroom teachers, doing everything from going to staff meetings to eating in the teachers' room to picketing with them. It's funny how the whole ESL program seems to gain validity as the ESL teacher becomes familiar. I've enjoyed the lunches in the teachers' room, and at least the shared slogging through agendas and puddles has given us common grounds for complaint.

---★---

That was a good meeting today. I really am thankful that I've become a high-visibility ESL person. Ever since we established the districtwide multicultural support group, all kinds of people bring their ideas and concerns to us and want to bounce them off the group to see what we think. Before I was the only "culture type," but now many others are helping me to share this role. It is very exciting, and it's happening without a tremendous amount of effort.

My hope is that the group will undertake a districtwide in-service training program to raise the consciousness of all staff members regarding multicultural issues. So far we haven't made any moves in this direction. To date we've worked principally with individual teachers or schools rather than trying to win over everyone at once.

But I'm pleased. At least the teachers I work with most are beginning to look beyond the exotic surface features of other cultures and are starting to explore ways to lead students to an understanding and, dare I say it? yes, an appreciation of cultural diversity. *E pluribus unum!*

---★---

Nonetheless, philosophical disagreements persist. Some mainstream teachers, especially those who teach young children, feel that it is unwarranted to take a student out of their classrooms for special instruction in English. Though they may have had no special training in second language pedagogy, they perceive themselves as fully qualified to deal with the linguistic needs of their non-English-background students. Administrators, who may also be poorly informed about the language needs of immigrant children (see chapter 7), will often side with the mainstream teacher when called in to mediate. You may be forced to accept what you know to be a less than ideal situation, suspecting that you will see the student in a year or two when the academic demands for language skills become more rigid.[1]

Sometimes the little ones are so attached to the mainstream teacher that they won't leave the classroom to work with me. They go so far as to latch on to the classroom teacher physically and loudly inform the world that they won't go with *her*, meaning *me*. Others seem to enjoy our time together and protest when they have to return to the regular classroom. I grow quite fond of many students as time goes by. It's sad to see them "graduate." Is being sentimental part of the job description?

In the afternoon things are going smoothly. I did have a run-in with the kindergarten teacher, though. She feels that the Vietnamese boy doesn't really need ESL because he is ready to read. She wanted to take him out of ESL entirely, and when I objected, she said, "Well, you know, what we do in kindergarten is important. . . . I suppose I could let you have him during snack."

We agreed that I would continue to take him, at the same time, three times a week (the schedule had worked out that I had him only four times anyhow). It took a certain amount of diplomacy.

Two conclusions emerge from that experience: first, if I have any kindergartners in the future, I should plan to have them come early in the day for ESL so that they don't miss any of the regular session. It would make life simpler for all concerned. Second, I've made a real mistake in trying to exit kids from the program too soon. I should have kept my Vietnamese boy this year—he might be doing better in his classes if I'd kept him. I had to take two Cambodians back for ESL support after I'd "graduated" them, and Alfredo is having trouble keeping up in his classes, too. One colleague suggested that the students who might need further ESL support are the ones making the big transitions—to the first grade, to the junior high or high school, and even to grades like third or fifth in the elementary school, in which a lot of new material is presented to the students.

The bottom line is that the exit evaluation is much more complex than I ever suspected. It is not just a matter of a test (standardized or teacher-made) of English structure; multiple criteria must be used and different skills should be weighted differently. The key really has to be, "What does it take to be successful in the mainstream classroom?"

──────── ★ ────────

In addition to disagreements about who should teach what, specific disagreements arise about teaching approaches or methodologies. Belief in teaching strategies is often as firm as belief in religious principles, and no concessions will be made.

──────── ★ ────────

Teachers in the Mainstream

I'm reminded daily of what a difference effective teaching styles can make in the lives of my students. One poor kid is suffering in a social studies class because the teaching strategy is to have the student use new vocabulary in sentences and provide definitions. It's particularly in cases like this that the ESL kids become frightened because they think that they have to get the exercise exactly right and they know that they are a million miles away from being a dictionary.

On the other hand, one girl is taking a history class in which the teacher is presenting each topic like a story or an allegory. I told the teacher that I felt that this strategy was particularly wonderful for ESL students from cultures in which storytelling is important, and that they would respond to this technique much better than to reading a textbook with bold type or similar materials. I thought she was right not to demand a lot from my student at this point about vocabulary but rather to try to get the story into the student's head. Later on the girl will learn the details.

───────── ★ ─────────

Similarly, a process approach to writing, in which students are expected to revise their work and in which content is valued over form, provokes resistance on the part of some product-oriented mainstream teachers, whose red pen, poised at the ready like a doctor's hypodermic needle, threateningly awaits the student who comes to turn in a paper. You will need to explain that your students are incapable of producing error-free compositions. If they could, they would be classified not as limited English proficient but as near-native speakers or writers, even though, as no doubt the mainstream teachers would agree, many native speakers fall far short of the mark when asked to produce a perfect piece of writing.

---- ★ ----

I had a funny experience today, and I realized my reaction was based on the pedagogical approach being taken. I've been sitting in on a fifth grader's language arts class that has really been annoying me. At the beginning of the year, the class was doing process writing. My student wrote a piece that needed some editing, but she did it, and the piece was in pretty good shape. The teachers weren't satisfied because they thought the class was falling short of achieving the teachers' learning objectives. Feeling that they needed to take a more direct approach to teaching mechanics, the teachers began to use a lot of work sheets and spend a lot of class time going over the compositions and correcting them. Next they progressed to paragraph writing by formula: write a topic sentence, write a concluding sentence, fill in the middle. Next they had the students string paragraphs together to focus on transitional sentences. Then, because of scheduling conflicts, I missed a couple of weeks. When I went in today, the teachers gave me a paper and told me my student needed a lot of help. "Could you help her get some transitional sentences?" they asked.

The piece was about milk. It did have five paragraphs but only because the student had indented periodically; there was no internal structure. The assignment had been to write five paragraphs of five sentences each using only ideas and information from one's head.

I became very angry and asked the student how she felt about the assignment. She said, "It's stupid," and I agreed. This was clearly a case of controlled writing gone amok. The teachers seemed to be punishing the kids with so-called traditional writing and holding out process writing as a reward.

I asked myself, how can I salvage something to help my student? I knew it would be counterproductive to launch an attack against my colleagues. I wrote a model composition for the kid using all the guidelines provided by the teacher. Then we read it together. Maybe she'll be able to write a composition of five paragraphs with five sentences each in the future, if she ever has to. I know she'll never want to.

———————★———————

Many mainstream teachers believe that a heavy dose of traditional grammar is all ESL students need to correct the situation. Some even seem unwilling to listen to the researchers who have demonstrated time after time that such is not the case; they seem not to consider their own experience, which surely indicates that writing improves only by studying writing, one's own and that of models, not by learning grammar rules in the abstract. They will not listen to you, whose training in psycholinguistics has no doubt taught you that errors are a natural part of the language learning process and disappear only when the learner has reached the appropriate stage of development, regardless of the amount of explicit grammar instruction in the interim.

What to do in the face of these conflicts? The central issue here is not which teaching philosophy is correct or better but how to maximize the learning experience for the language minority children. Clearly you will have to compromise, but not without retaining the right to counterbalance the mainstream teacher as the opportunity presents itself. Compromise means that if the ESL students have to turn in perfect compositions in their mainstream classes, then you will assist them in the preparation of such papers. You should also allow and encourage them to do some writing for their own benefit, writing in which they communicate what *they* want to say without concern for form until the final version is ready to be published. You should read authentic stories to your students and ask them to write real stories other students can read, and you should keep trying, in nonconfrontational ways, to be an agent for change in the school community.

I got into a heated discussion with a colleague today. I told her that an important part of my role was to teach my kids how to function in the U.S. educational system. But when I translated this to mean that I had to teach them how to grub for grades, she was taken aback. "What do you mean?" she challenged me. "The American way is to teach kids to value *learning*, not grades." I told her that it was demonstrably true that teachers' evaluation of students is highly subjective (no real objection here). Then I pointed out that a major factor in this subjective rating system is the degree to which a given student responds to teachers' expectations concerning classroom behaviors, academic as well as social. (Still no protest.) And then I said that many teachers are very subtle in passing on these expectations to the kids. The native English-speaking kids pick up the paralinguistic signals because they've been immersed in our communication system from birth. The ESL kids, in contrast, don't focus on the indirect suggestions, so I tell them exactly what they must do to make the teacher happy: eye contact, personal space, class participation, neatness, courtesy—all the little details that can make or break a kid. "In short," I said, "the key to academic success is to behave in a certain way." "Well," she said, "I always strive to be impartial in my grading." Just in case, I'll continue the coaching.

---- ★ ----

The old "who does what?" issue has surfaced again. Better said, the issue is "what do *I* do?" Last night it occurred to me that I would like one of my students to work on a dialogue journal.[2] This morning his English teacher informed me that she's already doing a journal with him! *Now* what do I do? A friend of mine suggested that I become an auxiliary writing teacher. I think I'll have the student show me the pieces he writes to fulfill assignments in his English class. Then we'll create a special-purpose journal just to work on these writings. It might be a better use of my time: I can respond to the writing quickly when I'm doing my preparations, then I'm free for other activities during class time. Also, the special journal will serve as a record of the work the student and I are doing together—good for reports of all types. Furthermore, in the past I've had a terrible time gaining access to the papers my students write in their regular classes, so it's tough for me to monitor their progress. By keeping a watch on the special journal, in conjunction with the portfolio I'll make of copies of the student's compositions, I'll be able to plan future lessons to help with revision and editing skills. I'm psyched! Write on!

---- ★ ----

My students' emotional ups and downs are a side of my job that I continue to wrestle with. Throughout the year at one time or another I need to find out a student's wavelength by asking, "How's it going?" "What's the problem here?" My very best student is in a blue funk right now about her grades. She's having a terrible time in English because the class is doing critical skills work and she doesn't like the way the students are working or not working together. Furthermore, she didn't tell me she was having problems with *A Tale of Two Cities*. What pleased me was the way the girl was working on her conflicts. She had shared some frustrations with me a week before, and the next thing I knew, her English teacher sought me out to say that the girl had disappeared from his class. Trying to make her feel better, I called the girl up at work that Friday afternoon to tell her that she had passed a district writing competency she had been depressed about. She said, "I went to see my English teacher today to talk to him about the class." I thought, "She's miserable, but she went to the teacher and talked to him." That's something right there. To teach them—to get them—to talk to the teachers is so valuable. In spite of how miserable she was, I was already feeling happy to think, "She's dealing with it. She's not talking just to me about it, she's talking to her other teachers."

---- ★ ----

It's wonderful to see people grow. I have noticed in the last few weeks that a first grade teacher I have been working with has become much more caring toward one of the ESL students: the girl sits on her lap and clings to her often. And I hear so many more positive things from the teacher about the student! I sense that the girl was too foreign for the teacher at first. I've spent half a year telling this teacher, "Look, this girl is getting used to school. She is one of the few kids you have who has never been to school, and, besides, she lives in a different first language environment." I don't know if the teacher began to see things from this perspective or not, but something has happened. I have discovered that the teachers have to feel comfortable with the students. When they don't, the students become *my* problem.

In a sense that responsibility is one of the great aspects of this job. In fact, I've had teachers come up to me and say, "I know sometimes you feel inadequate or wonder what you're doing, but you are an advocate for these students. You are here for them; the day your position is gone, these students will have lost their advocate; the longer you're here, the more you develop this sense of advocacy in other teachers." And that is true. It is the wonderful thing about crossing the grade levels the way I do. I build up my group of advocates in the different schools and promote the students when I talk to my colleagues. Little by little, they pick up part of my responsibility.

───────── ★ ─────────

Teachers in the Mainstream

An important part of what I do is to function as an intermediary. I take some of the foreignness off and make other teachers feel they can handle the student with my help.

One of the teachers at the elementary school did not expect to have a non-English-speaking Vietnamese student dropped into her class halfway through the year, and she asked me to stop by after school every few days to check in with her. Every time I do so, she says anxiously, "I've tried something with Nguyen, and I don't know if it's all right. . . ." So far she has matched him up with a classmate for reading, found a friend to help him get used to the cafeteria, given him a job handing out materials, and put up a big map of Vietnam on the wall. He showed the class where he came from, and they put a star on the place. Every time I see the class going to one of the special instructional activities (art, music, gym), he's with someone, a real part of the group. Her latest worry was, "He took his lunch bag and blew it up and popped it, and I scolded him. I don't know if I was right. He's been so good that I was worried, so I was really delighted that he acted up a little bit, but on the other hand, I thought I ought to treat him the way I do the other students. Was it all right?" Was it all right?! She's doing such a marvelous, creative job of helping Nguyen feel at home that it's a pleasure for me to talk with her. I've noticed that the other students in her class seem both caring and comfortable with him. She responds, "But this is such a special, wonderful class. Of course they're great with him." The other teachers say that she says that every year.

My theory is that a teacher who works well with the ESL children is probably a very good teacher in general. One of the

Chapter 6

nice things about my job is being able to cheer on people who are doing a good job!

--- ★ ---

I still remember one of the most problematic students I have ever had. He had always been a problem for his family too, and all the teachers except a couple of Special Education people and a shop instructor had written him off. I defended this student and worked with him year after year. Now he has a good job and is a respectable citizen.

It is very rewarding for me to be able to go back to the other teachers and report on my former students' successes. That helps me to gain credibility and consequently to build my constituency.

--- ★ ---

I have to make the mainstream teachers feel comfortable. I think that most teachers are smart enough to see that they should stop doing something that is wholly inappropriate. But for me to say to them categorically that they should not use this or that strategy doesn't work. I have to compromise with teachers whose approach is different from mine. I have to let them take some initiatives and then give them some ideas to make their instruction more appropriate because, after all, they *are* carrying the burden, and, initially, they feel the responsibility of making sure the student is doing something that seems productive to them. I have to keep reminding them that it takes time to develop proficiency in a second language. Besides, it's tough for the ESL students to be in an intense instructional setting all day long in a new language environment. They need some down time, too. I figure some traditional activities probably won't do much good, but they won't do much damage either, and in the long run I'll reach my goals without causing a lot of hard feelings along the way.

At the elementary level I'm spending some of my time in the classroom working alongside the other teachers. My role has become one of recording behavior, alerting the teacher to various aspects of the behavior, and sketching out the situation for the teacher: "This is where I think the student is. He's making progress, and these are the things that we need to look at."

I've been working with a girl in the readiness program. A couple of times her teacher has said to me, "I can't do it now, but in the second half of the year I'll probably try to get her out to Chapter I, and they'll do that individual work with her." Most students profit from individualized attention, and it usually works out very well. The point I wanted to make with her is that the student is making great progress in her classroom right now, but at her own pace. You can see real growth compared with a month or two ago. And now I'm beginning to see how she learns. Her style actually parallels that of another child in her family in that she's very much an auditory learner. When I arrive in the classroom, the teacher looks crestfallen and says, "Oh, my God, when will this student ever write a story or know her sound-symbol relationships?" Then I go to the practice session for an art, music, and gym spectacular for readiness and grade one, and this student is doing a great job; she knows all the words of the songs by heart.

I must be a cheerleader for these students. I always have to point out what skill the student is excelling in right now. If the student is excelling in auditory and oral work, I have to say so and point out how that success will lead to success in the other areas.

───── ★ ─────

You and the mainstream teachers must work together in a spirit of cooperation. To do otherwise undermines the teaching effort of the school and ultimately affects the learning outcomes vis-à-vis the language minority students. Our experience has shown that, fortunately, the consciousness raising you will have to do just to survive nearly always results in understanding on the part of the mainstream teachers and, if not approval, at least professional respect.

───── ★ ─────

I just can't figure it out. I know Hana isn't a "B" student but she didn't deserve an "F" either. Why can't people be more objective?

It all started because a couple of my high school students had to take a required computer course—a new state mandate. The teacher wasn't at all happy because he was told that from then on the course would be a service course, open to all comers, and there would be no homogeneous grouping. I could sense there might be trouble, so I wrote a long letter to the teacher explaining the background of my two students and asking the teacher to contact me at once if their work was not up to par.

Toward the end of the quarter, I got a note from the teacher saying Hana would be getting an "F". I was furious, first, because the teacher had waited so long to contact me and, second, because I had been working with Hana on her assignments and I thought she understood the material quite well. As soon as I was free I went over to the computer science department and asked for an explanation. I pointed out that all my work with Hana had led me to believe that she deserved at least a passing grade. After mumbling something about Hana not saying much in class, the teacher said he'd have to think about it and get back to me. I heard not a word from him. Today Hana came in to tell me she got a "B" in computer studies. She was thrilled, and I wanted to share her joy, but inside I was boiling. Hana probably deserved only a "C". What made me angry was that the teacher made no attempt to do a fair evaluation. He reacted to my challenge by taking the easy way out.

Teachers in the Mainstream

---

*I*t was a real blow to some of my students when they first came up from the middle school and started falling off the honor roll. I understand how they feel, so I'm very careful to tell all their classroom teachers that I want to know immediately if any of my students is failing. I can usually provide extra help, have the teacher changed, and so on. Some of my students are willing to take an "F" and repeat the course, but I encourage them to look for ways to be successful the first time. Success is *so* important to their self-concept.

There are obstacles sometimes. For example, I recall a student who had received passing grades all term. I never considered that he might fail, but it turned out that the grades were assigned based on work and tests the student had done with the help of a resource room teacher, one who had a reputation for feeding the answers to the students. I don't believe she actually did that; I think she was just bending over backward to get the student to produce the correct answer, making many allowances to be sure. She conducted the tests with a lot of give-and-take discussion, a far cry from the type of exercises the mainstream teacher was utilizing. When the mainstream teacher tried to evaluate the student without the presence of the resource room teacher, the results were very poor.

The mainstream teacher had not developed a good rapport with the student, so the boy was very nervous. The grade was so bad that the mainstream teacher actually tried to nullify all the grades she had written on the student's papers—grades that were most likely already posted in her rank book.

In truth, the student was probably neither as good as the resource room teacher had reported nor as bad as the mainstream teacher was prepared to claim. In my view, the teacher had no right to nullify the grades already assigned. To do so would serve only to punish the student, who had no responsibility for the possible error in evaluation.

In contrast, I sometimes see students who appear, as far as what their teachers say, to be at the norm of their classes, yet as far as I can see they clearly have some problems that I might try to address.

―――――★―――――

Sometimes teachers say, "I don't know why this student is taking ESL. He's doing so well in my class." I've thought about this comment a lot. In part it must be due to different standards of evaluation—of academic rigor, to use the jargon, or perhaps different expectations that place fewer demands on language minority students than on others. This attitude could be related to the cognitive level of class activities and evaluations as well. Maybe I'm asking for performance higher up on the scale than my colleagues are.

The art teacher at the elementary school has taken an interest in one of my fourth graders for some time. We've arranged that I will give up some of my ESL time, she will give up one of her lunches each week, and we'll work together with this girl. The student has been excited about it, even though we had to put off her first class for a week. In her journal yesterday she wrote:

"What is your favorite thing to do in Art when we go to Art tomorrow because I like to watch you draw in art and I know that I never see you drawing before but I will tomorrow see your drawing."

The art teacher fooled her, though. She has started the student decorating a white shirt with colored ribbon. The teacher said, "This is art," and the student was willing to accept that it was. Meanwhile the student is doing a meticulous job of sewing, totally centered and at peace with herself, which is what she needs.

What is most exciting for me is to watch the art teacher specifically welcoming the student into one of Frank Smith's clubs[3]—the club of artists—and she does so, defining artists as follows: "We make mistakes, and we use them. We try different ways of looking at a problem. We don't define what we do narrowly; we don't just draw, but we sew as well. We are patient with long-term projects. We get good ideas that we may not use 'til later."

It was also very refreshing to see that the art teacher could recognize this girl's obvious artistic gifts and, overlooking her linguistic deficiencies, work with her in a creative and productive way.

★

Like the language minority students, you will be perceived as an outsider, a little-understood intruder into the U.S. school system. You will need the support and cooperation of the mainstream teachers both for your own morale and for the success of your academic program. Your duties, your philosophy of teaching and learning, and your sense of responsibility will often bring you into conflict with the mainstream teaching staff. The challenge, then, will be to win over your colleagues by modeling, advocacy, and diplomacy. Initially mainstream teachers will either expect too much of you or refuse to accept your assistance at all, but in time they will come to understand that you, the professional oddball, merit their respect and support.

Notes

1. See the discussion of academic language proficiency in chapter 1.
2. A *dialogue journal* is a notebook in which student and teacher write back and forth to each other about learning and feelings about learning.

3. The *club* is a notion proposed by language arts authority Frank Smith (1986), who argues that, to perform like other club members, individuals must feel a sense of belonging and know the rules by having been initiated. The teacher functions as the initiator-inductor.

chapter seven

Administrators, or Who Is My Boss, Anyway?

FOCUSING QUESTIONS

★ How do ESL programs relate to the standard curriculum?

★ What positive and negative effects does the typical administrative structure have on the ESL program?

★ Why is evaluation of ESL teachers and programs difficult for administrators?

★ How do school boards influence ESL programs?

★ Why is it difficult for ESL teachers to arrange for substitutes?

★ What is the toughest battle ESL teachers have with administrators? Why?

★ What nonteaching duties do administrators typically assign to ESL teachers?

★ Who typically designs the job description for ESL teachers?

The chain of command in public school ESL programs is often difficult to establish, and it will usually be you, the ESL teacher, who ends up clarifying the situation. In the small ESL programs discussed here, often the assistant superintendent or districtwide curriculum coordinator is assigned to oversee ESL operations. This arrangement has both advantages and disadvantages for you. On the one hand, the heavy work load of top-level administrators means that they will tend to give you a free hand in setting up your program. They virtually never interfere in day-to-day operations, and evaluation is mostly pro forma. On the other hand, it is difficult to arrange for support when you need it, again because the heavy schedule of the supervisor usually means that the relatively tiny ESL program has to wait its turn for attention.

─── ★ ───

The secretary asked, "By the way, who's your boss? Nobody seems to know, and nobody really claims you."

─── ★ ───

We don't have a policy on evaluation of the ESL teacher and the program, so I've arranged to meet with the assistant superintendent to set one.

─── ★ ───

I think I have the flu, but I went in to meet with my boss anyway on setting up an evaluation plan for the ESL program. I had pulled out every article I had on evaluation (not much, and mostly on program evaluation rather than teacher evaluation) and was able to summarize them for him, but he was on a slightly different tack. We agreed to work on the basis of this preliminary discussion and to meet again.

───── ★ ─────

I was initially hired because an extended family of Afghans with no English had arrived to join the large extended family of Cambodians with no English. I was nervous the first time I was evaluated because I knew that not only my job but the existence of the ESL program depended on my impressing my supervisor, so I prepared as well as I could.

I was trying cross-age grouping at that time. The idea was that the older students would do seat work while I used the *I Love English* series (Capelle, Pavlik, & Segal, 1985) with the younger ones, the younger ones would work on their own while I worked with the older students, and they'd come together for stories and cultural activities. I still think it was a good idea, but it wasn't working very well at that point. It sometimes takes a while for everyone to accept the ground rules. The Cambodian students, who had spent less than a year in the school in the refugee camp, tended to bounce off the walls and swing from the light fixtures if I didn't constantly keep on their cases. The Afghani boy resented being placed with his sisters and female cousins and sulked. The older girls were trying hard to deal with the conflict between the traditional ways their mothers expected of them and what their classroom teachers wanted. The younger girl had clearly been told to behave herself or else. But we were beginning to fit together. Josefa and Alix would occasionally play with the puppets together, or at least at the same time, and Melisa was beginning to speak out loud occasionally. Even Omar was starting to relax.

Then the supervisor came in. Melisa and her cousin grabbed their veils, which they had dropped on the floor, and looked around for a place to hide from this tall American man. Omar parked himself in front of my supervisor, trying to get all of his attention. I told Melisa, her cousin, and Omar to get going on the writing we'd begun earlier and grabbed the younger children to read from their books.

Alix said, "*I Love English?* No, no, I hate English!" Josefa, delighted at this joke, announced even louder, "I hate English! Everybody hates English!" Giggling, they went through a list of everyone they knew who hated English.

---★---

*I*t had to happen. In our conversation following my supervisor's observation, he asked me how I set my priorities for teaching. I felt like using that old Eisenhower line, "Give me a week to think about it," but that was not a realistic option, as I'm not anxious to find myself among the unemployed. I dug deep and decided that in spite of my usual nonchalance, I do have a system in place. Knowing that my boss was not familiar with the intricacies of ESL programs, I responded with generalities about preparing students to function in the mainstream classes. Assuming that he would assume I knew how to do that, I didn't get into specifics. I told him how much I emphasize U.S. culture in my program—administrators are always anxious for rapid acculturation, if not assimilation, to take place.

I didn't sermonize, but I think I made my boss see that there was a reasonable plan behind what may have seemed to be disconnected activities. But I still don't think I'll write it down.

---★---

I have to write a self-evaluation for my personnel file, so I figured I might as well reread my supervisor's observation reports. I always get a little tense when he tells me he's coming in. Because he's so unfamiliar with my field, he must think some of the stuff we do is off the wall. I would feel uncomfortable at the thought that I'm "doing band-aids." Although I acknowledge that what happens on any given day in my classroom may look like a sudden response to an immediate impulse or even look chaotic, I do hope my lesson plan is guided by a feel for what the students are going to need both in school and out.

--- ★ ---

School boards can be particularly frustrating. Made up mostly of noneducators, they may have absolutely no idea what is involved in meeting the needs of language minority students. During the discussion of the need for an ESL program, school board members will often recite tales of relatives or friends who came to the United States speaking no English and who, with no special help, were fluent in their new language in just a few weeks. These stories cannot be true, but there is no way to convince the storytellers otherwise, and they insist on immersing the children in the mainstream classrooms.

Only when the superintendent brings to the board's attention that state and federal laws require special language instruction for all students unable to function at grade level without it do school board members reluctantly back down. Even then, school board members have been known to challenge the term *English as a second language*, claiming that "in the United States English is the *first* language, and we're not going to do anything in *this* school district to indicate otherwise."

Many ESL teachers would like to see second language instruction begin in preschool (at 3 years of age, similar to special education programs) so that the students could be mainstreamed by grade one. This would cost extra money initially, so school boards tend to respond negatively to the idea.

★

Cost effectiveness is a constant frustration for me. It's obvious to me that I have fewer students than a regular classroom teacher does, but most teachers stay in the same room all day, whereas I have to shuttle back and forth among three schools. Besides, the mainstream teachers all deal with students who are at pretty much the same grade level. My students are all levels, from age 5 to age 19, not to mention their varying English proficiency and overall ability levels. So why shouldn't I have an aide, or at least a tutor? But I can't justify the expense to the board's satisfaction, so I guess I'll have to start working with peer tutors. Some of my students need a lot of individual help. I'd like to work with them myself, but they're locked into schedules that conflict with mine. I hate to pull them out of classes where they're having some success.

★

My supervisor called me today. He wanted to know if I would teach during the summer, as he had found some extra funds and thought it would be good to maintain some continuity. Good? It would be great! My students have so little exposure to English. They spend nearly all their time with their non-English-speaking families. I think it's great that a group of sponsors has organized the weeklong camps for teenagers, but they run only for a week, and they cost so much—the sponsors have to spend all year on fund raising! And there's nothing for the younger students.

The students need ESL in the summer, but I need a break. I just can't do it without burning out. A hired tutor wouldn't even have to be very knowledgeable about ESL. It would be fine with me if the tutor worked only on vocabulary development. I suggested this option to my supervisor but couldn't think of anyone to recommend. I'll have to try hard to come up with someone. After all, he's got the money, and it will make my job much easier next fall. Maybe it could be a high school student.

───── ★ ─────

When classroom teachers need to be absent for a day or more, their replacement is rather straightforward: the substitute teacher consults the standardized lesson plans and implements them. In contrast, replacing an absent ESL teacher is much more complex because of the highly individualized nature of the instruction and the typical need to travel to more than one building.

I don't know what to do. I have to be out for 3 days next week, and my supervisor thinks I should get a sub. For what? First of all, the mind boggles at trying to explain how the schedule works, how to find the student, how to find where you're working with the student on any particular day, and what you're doing with each student. Even if the sub understood it, she'd never be able to make all the connections. How many times, with the limited amount of time that you have, can you write up the right little sentences that are going to cue the sub into how to deal with your students? Every time I've known ahead of time that I was going to be absent, I've spent 3 hours writing up a day for the sub, especially if I didn't know who it was going to be. I always ask myself, "When in the heck is this person going to read this stuff? She'll never have time to read it!"

Having a sub come in "cold" is like playing Russian roulette. They called in a "cold" sub one time when I was sick. It didn't work at all. All she did was lecture to the students. She told me she didn't think the students were able to do anything!

The students tell me they hate the subs, and sometimes they tell me why. They say the subs tell them things like, "You're never going to make it if you don't do this." The fact is the sub has to coexist with the students for 50 minutes. She needs to be able to get some positive interaction going by coming up with interesting discussion topics.

But it's tough for a substitute teacher. This year I'm working in the regular classroom with a couple of students. How can I ask the sub to go in there and sit down and work with a student? On the other hand, how can I ask the sub to drag the student out when I never drag the student out?

If I have to find a substitute, I want to be sure she is carefully screened. Then I'll have to make especially detailed lesson plans because it makes both the students and the sub feel secure. I'll also set up maps and charts, and I'll have some notes on the students' personalities as well as information about their other classes. I think it's better to forewarn subs rather than force them to discover everything for themselves. And I'll give the sub some totally new material—I'll look through my supplementary, high-interest stuff. I guess I'll make up a week's worth of lesson plans that can be plugged in at any time and leave them on my desk. Reading a good book always works, and so do free writing and the ideas in *Talk-A-Tivities* (Yorkey, 1985) or *Recipes for Tired Teachers* (Sion, 1985). I'll also ask the sub to write up a report about what she did. That should do it!

───────── ★ ─────────

Perhaps the toughest battle in dealing with administrators is the search for space in which to house the ESL program. The building principal might consider you as an appendage to his staff, not an integral part. If so, all other staff requests for space will probably be filled before your needs are considered. As a result, closets, hallways, cubbyholes under stairways, and shared classrooms are often the learning centers for the language minority students. Often there is little if any space for storage of materials, which in any case need to be transportable as you more than likely will have to see students in two or more schools during each workday. Another problem might be the lack of a noise-free or properly lighted and ventilated space. Interruptions and distractions will be frequent. It is important for the ESL program to have a space where activities can be spread out and where the class can be noisy at times—such as when doing a Total Physical Response (TPR) activity. What to do?

———————★———————

Another day and a half fitted into one day. I discovered that the new speech therapist had arrived and taken possession of my room, "but I'm only here Tuesdays and Wednesdays."

How do I solve the Tuesday-Wednesday problem? On Tuesdays, at least, there is no room for us. That means the hallway for two separate groups and no place to put anything, no chalkboard, and certainly no way to use the tape recorder or do any very physical TPR activities—not with people walking through all the time. Wednesdays my aide and I can fight for the conference room, and the loser gets the hall. How can we teach under those circumstances?

---- ★ ----

*T*hings haven't worked out too badly. The counselor's room is free Tuesdays, and the conference room on Wednesdays, so only one group has to use the hall. I've been doing reading with the second graders there on Tuesdays. They love finding little niches and hiding under the tables to read, so it isn't too bad.

---- ★ ----

Given these challenges, you will have to investigate all possibilities to improve your housing. You should make friends with janitors, who always seem to know about interesting options; you should urge mainstream teachers who seem to have a surplus of space to share with you, perhaps in return for a professional service, and failing in these attempts, you should go up the administrative chain of command until your needs are met, realizing that animosity may result. As always, you should act to benefit your program and the students it serves.

As a result of the lack of direct involvement of administrators in the education of the language minority children, you will usually have to complete surveys and reports required by the school district, the state, or the federal government. Although you generally will have the data requested, completing this administrative work will place an extra burden on you. You usually will not have much planning time during the day. You will need to schedule in the various groups or individuals when you can, nearly always a complicated task; there is also the question of travel time between schools, including knockdown and setup of materials and audiovisual equipment. You must therefore do planning and paperwork at home. If you don't complete the reports as requested, your program and the students it serves could be jeopardized by budget cutbacks or elimination.

---------★---------

Yikes! I have to turn in my end-of-the-year reports soon. I began thinking about them the other day and realized I haven't done much formal testing this year. I used to test constantly—I begged or borrowed fancy testing kits and came up with crazy scores that looked really impressive: José is a 3.2 on the HAP-LES scale, and so on. But this year, aside from a few tentative forays with tests from the state ESL consultant, I've done no testing at all. What I have done is to keep a lot of the students' work in portfolios and a daily record of everything we do in class with notes about individual performance. I know how each student is coping with mainstream courses, and I know each student's grades, so I think I'm pretty much on top of monitoring progress. The only real test of the effectiveness of my instruction is whether the students can function adequately in the regular program. Where there are deficiencies is where I put my effort. My reports this year will look different, but they'll have much more meaning. I hope my supervisor appreciates that.

---★---

I recently got a survey from the State Department of Education asking for data on the non-English-background population of all schools in the district. In the past, I used to provide all the information myself, but this year the state wanted each building principal to complete the survey personally. In fact, the state wanted the principals to do so in the past as well, but all the forms ended up on my desk anyway. Twenty-eight pages of repetitious statistics! And they wonder why I feel burned out at times. Anyway, this year I spent a lot of time running around trying to get all the principals to do it. Apparently, a few took the state's charge seriously and completed the survey for their school, so I couldn't do it for the whole district. I was forced to chase around and ask the others, "Have you done it yet? Can I help you?"

The good side of all that trouble is that the state is trying to raise the consciousness of the supervising principals—making them think about services to students from non-English backgrounds. For me it's a pain in the neck, but it does give me an opportunity to educate the administrators and to remind them of their responsibilities under the law. Fortunately, they do respond positively over time.

---★---

You will most likely draw up your own job description. When asked by an administrator to prepare such a document, you should be careful to ask for the opportunity to revise after you have experienced most of the challenges and requests for services that are apt to come up. In this way you can develop a list of responsibilities in line with your professional priorities and your capacity to carry them out in a reasonable time frame. You can also argue for assistance if the work load justifies it, and, quite importantly, you can use the document to educate your colleagues, administrators, and school board members about your function in the academic program of the school district. The job description should explain the comprehensive, multifaceted role of the ESL teacher.

---★---

At long last, I arranged with my supervisor to hire an ESL associate. The difference between aides and associates is that associates get paid a little more. I always put in for an associate, on the official basis that the person has to be good enough to work without direct immediate supervision; unofficially I'm embarrassed at asking someone to work for even the little more money an associate earns. After we put an ad in the paper, I was worried about finding time to interview people and train the lucky winner. As luck would have it, a couple of acquaintances were taking a course at the College, and the name *Chomsky*[1] came up. They immediately thought of me and invited me over to explain what *Chomsky* was. One of them became interested in hearing about ESL and asked if he could observe a class. After doing so, he applied for the job, thinking that it looked like fun. For me it's marvelous! He will work two periods a day with my Vietnamese students and one period, I think, on computers if I can find a couple of them free. I have two sets of software, so the students can work on different activities, which will take some of the competitive pressure off.

———————— ★ ————————

Today I went in to see my boss with all my notes from the state consultant's 4-day workshop last spring and said, "Look, I have all this material here. I can order the Language Assessment Scales (LAS) testing materials from McGraw-Hill; I can do this, and I can do that." Do you know what he said? "Do you really need to do any of that? I've looked at the records and found that district students have already had hours and hours of tests. Furthermore, *you* know these students better than anyone else. *You* can decide on their placement!" I thought I'd die. Here I was ready to be superprofessional—after all, I do have a testing and measurement background with years of working in that field, and I had the specimen set of the LAS. Now I guess we're back in the boat of "Mama Knows Best!" I don't feel uncomfortable with this as long as the students are comfortable, but no doubt the very next administrator will think differently.

---★---

Lee had dropped out of school in September with (we thought) one class to go before graduation, but when the principal and I went through his records, it turned out that Lee had more than enough credits to graduate. He didn't have to come back to study after all. I asked if he could have his diploma before next June (the administration's first proposal; after all, it's embarrassing for them to "lose" a graduate), and the administration came through beautifully.

We set up an appointment for Lee to come in and get his diploma from the principal, and I planned to leave class and take a picture. The principal's secretary found a cap and gown and got someone to take pictures.

Lee arrived a few minutes early, wearing a suit and tie. I took him down to the main office, and we helped him into the cap and gown. He saw a substitute teacher he knows in the next office, so we invited him to join us. Lee's guidance counselor came over, and the other teacher stood on a chair and took several pictures as the principal shook Lee's hand, posed (intentionally?) in front of the U.S. flag. I felt a bit teary eyed.

Afterwards, Lee came up and sat in my room to talk for a while. He kept patting the diploma and saying, "Now, if I want to go to college—of course, I *don't* want to go to college, I need to work—but if I *want* to go to college, no one can stop me."

Lee's picture and a little write-up were printed in the local newspapers, and the substitute teacher is giving him a frame for his diploma. The secretary made sure he kept the tassel to put on his rearview mirror.

I love the way they all came through for him—without my prodding.

---★---

You, as the ESL teacher, must understand the challenges you will face from the various levels of supervision. Most administrators will not know what you are supposed to do or how you should do it. They will rely on you both to do your job with minimal direction and to keep them informed so that they may provide their publics with satisfactory answers to questions raised. They will watch your program numbers closely, raise questions about productivity, and suggest cutbacks and economizing when the budget crunch is on. Administrators will depend on you to keep state and federal authorities happy by submitting reports and program descriptions. They might even expect you to interpret for them the laws and policies governing the education of language minority children. School boards will want to hear from you regarding the nature of and need for your program. You will most likely need to campaign for board support through the sponsor network. These responsibilities are added to your seemingly unending list.

Note

1. Massachusetts Institute of Technology linguist Noam Chomsky, considered the father of modern linguistic inquiry.

chapter eight

Nurses and Guidance Counselors

FOCUSING QUESTIONS

★ How does the ESL teacher become involved in questions of health and hygiene?

★ How does the ESL teacher support the school nurse?

★ What are the pitfalls of serving as counselor to language minority students?

★ How can the ESL teacher assist guidance counselors in working with language minority children?

★ What role can the ESL teacher play in college counseling? What conflicts might develop?

Dealing with illness among the language minority students is another challenge you will face. Nearly every aspect of the situation differs from the typical scenario involving non-ESL students. In the first place, some immigrant children are sent to school when they should be at home in bed. Cultural attitudes toward illness vary widely among different ethnic groups, so a child from a non-English background most likely has not learned to describe pain or other discomforts in the same ways as his native English-speaking peers are accustomed to do. Moreover, in many cases the child does not have the vocabulary to describe symptoms, and determining the cause of discomfort becomes a guessing game. It is virtually obligatory that you accompany your students on visits to the school nurse. Although possessed of the best intentions, the school nurse often has had no training in dealing with language minority patients. Like many other Americans, the nurse may be unprepared to communicate with a child from a non-English background and may try increasing the volume of speech, reducing the speed to a very exaggerated degree, and using baby talk.

★

This morning I had to take a student to the nurse. The poor kid had a crashing headache, but the nurse had to check on what else might be wrong and went into a hilarious basic English routine: "How's your stomach? Feeling queasy? Does she understand me? Do-you-understand? Do-you-need-to-throw-up? If-you-need-to-vomit-tell-me. I'll-get-a-basin-if-you-want-to-upchuck." I managed to restrain myself and asked my student with gestures if she was sick to her stomach, and she said, "No. Only head," and we finally got her a Tylenol.

★

The school nurse may transfer many of the assumptions she makes about native English-speaking children to her language minority clients. For instance, she may assume that they can identify common ailments such as headache or stomachache and that other cultural groups define illness and wellness as those in the mainstream U.S. culture do. And she may assume that minorities would explain the causes of illness as she would explain them. None of these assumptions is valid, and it will fall to you once again to be both interpreter and cultural mediator.

---★---

A student had been withdrawn all morning, hiding behind his hair and writing very faintly. A few minutes later he asked, "What do you do for a bad stomachache . . . since ten-thirty last night . . . like you want to throw up?"

I decided it sounded more like stress than anything else, offered sympathy, and recommended Alka-Seltzer.

---★---

When parental permission is needed for medication or other treatment, it will be you who will explain the rationale for such procedures. During these contacts you will expand your repertoire of culturally diverse explanations for breakdowns in bodily functions. You will learn to assume nothing, to listen carefully, and to prepare your questions and comments thoughtfully.

---★---

Chapter 8

How do I communicate to my Southeast Asian parents my concern about their children's health? How do I explain about colds? When the students get sick, the parents don't really understand it. On one level they seem to understand the relationship between the cold weather and illness. They say, "Oh, with this cold weather we always get sick," but they don't take the next step and analyze why *they get sick. One of the reasons my students get sick—I know this for a fact—is that the parents don't want to spend money on oil and thus keep the house too cold. They're used to other explanations of illness: drinking dirty water, being bitten by mosquitoes, or getting sick because of a ghost in the tree, but in their culture you don't get sick from being cold.*

───────── ★ ─────────

Your involvement with the sick child will not end with the initial diagnosis and treatment. Unlike the family doctor, you will likely make a house call to check on the progress of students recuperating from illness or accident. If the student is able to do some schoolwork, you should prepare special lessons and either personally deliver the assignments or communicate them by phone. If necessary, you might provide transportation for visits to the doctor or trips to the drugstore. In sum, although you do not replace the school nurse in her central function, you will extend the health service far beyond the school walls, usually with the active help and support of the school nurse.

Although she may not fully understand the implications of linguistic and cultural differences, the school nurse is just as helpful in attending to the medical needs of the language minority students as she is in caring for other students. She monitors their inoculation schedules, arranges for other medications and remedies, and in general is very supportive of the ESL program.

★

We've been doing a unit on "What the Student Health Services Can Do for You" plus a grammatical focus on compound nouns. Today I wanted the students to do some writing and, if we had time, one of the compound noun games. Most of what we've been doing is prewriting activities, so I gave the students a statement on the relative merits of home remedies, over-the-counter drugs, and prescription medicines. They wrote brainstorm lists, then webs, then first drafts. They shared the first drafts, made additions and deletions, then handed them over to me for spelling and grammar checks. I thought it was a neat way to integrate my curriculum with the Health Program.

★

Chapter 8

*E*ver wondered what sex is like in a second language? My ninth graders are learning all about it in health class. To reinforce the learning, I have to drill them on the vocabulary. We put all the terms on the board and practice pronunciation and definitions. They're pretty good at it; much better than I expected given the length and difficulty of the technical terminology. But they are also into street language, and they always want to know how the words they learn at play relate to the sterile lexicon they get in school. I close the door to avoid scandals from overheard Anglo-Saxonisms or eyebrows raised at the graphic terminology and drawings displayed on my chalkboard and take up the challenge of teaching "dangerous English." I try to explain everything fully and point out that proper usage means differentiation by time, place, and audience. They have no sense of the emotional content of taboo words in English, but they can learn some simple rules of register. My older students are tougher, however. One insists on trying to shock me with his earthy comments. I thought I had him somewhat under control, but the other day he showed me he was just waiting for the proper moment to strike. Another student was sitting slouched down in his chair with a heavy jacket bulged way out over his stomach. My risqué raconteur observed this and said, "You look like pregnant yak." I laughed in spite of myself and then said, "I'm not sure that's an appropriate way to comment about a fellow student," and he answered, "Why you laugh then?" I did think it was rather imaginative.

Nurses and Guidance Counselors

Not all health-related responsibilities are fun, however.

This afternoon I spent some time with the public health nurse working out the best time for tuberculosis testing of a family of one of my students. I hope the results will be negative, but that's unlikely.

Guidance counselors present a varied response to the language minority students as well. Those counselors who see their function as primarily assisting in the selection of colleges or career paths show little interest in working with children who, in many cases, are not going to be following in the footsteps of their U.S.-born classmates. Nonetheless, many language minority students excel academically and, by the time they are seniors in high school, are qualified to apply to college, some to highly selective ones. Other counselors, who are more interested in the affective development of the students, do at times attempt to counsel ESL students, trying to help them deal with the many frustrations and disappointments they must confront on a daily basis.

Cross-cultural counseling requires special skills. Although you may not have had special training in counseling, you probably will have had a great deal of exposure to cultural differentiation and to the conflicts that result when two diverse cultures come into contact. This background will make you better prepared than the guidance staff, in most cases, to deal with the language minority children. Many guidance counselors will recognize this and will refer any requests for counseling involving children from non-English backgrounds to you. Once again you will be faced with a dilemma: you will want to help the child, but you will probably feel unprepared to deal with many types of problems, especially severe emotional disorders. Furthermore, you might wonder how you can fit another time-consuming task into an already overloaded schedule. You should resist the pressures to perform this function; after all, it is not your job. Nonetheless, you will sometimes find yourself heavily involved with the emotional lives of one or more students.

After attempting to handle all the counseling yourself and finding that you cannot keep up with the caseload, you will probably realize that you must put your energy into developing a cooperative relationship with the guidance staff. By spending a few productive minutes instructing the guidance counselor on a few cultural basics, as well as on the idiosyncrasies of the student in question, you will be able to free up much of your time to deal with your other responsibilities. You cannot drop the counseling role completely; through dialogue journals and private conversations you will monitor the progress of the student, and you should contact the guidance counselor frequently to request updates.

———★———

Today I went down to the counselor's office. She greeted me almost hysterically. "I think Jon had a psychotic break a couple of weeks ago. You know the kind of pressure he's been under, with his family conflicts and being an illegal alien and all. Well, he came in and told me about dabbling in devil worshipping and that sort of thing." "Could he be doing drugs?" I asked myself. We agreed that if anyone deserves to have a situational psychosis, it's Jon, but she pointed out that schizophrenia tends to show up in 16- or 17-year-olds and that maybe he's a victim.

We turned the situation around and around without finding a solution. If Jon were only here legally, we could get Youth Services in on it. He could get a job, a driver's license, even an apartment if necessary. He could certainly get mental health help.

I also mentioned that he has a "D" in ESL and an "F" in Economics. She answered that he was doing the same in all his courses and that she just couldn't worry about it at this point. We didn't resolve anything, though we agreed that we'd do our best to keep Jon alive, in school, and on as good terms as possible with his family until his father can become a citizen. It may become possible for him to become one, too.

― ★ ―

Today I took my grades down to the office and confirmed that a student who had been out with an injury will get grades and not incompletes for ESL and Economics. I made an appointment with another student's counselor for tomorrow. He told me that the student's guardian had deserted him and that maybe it was just as well, because the guardian was an alcoholic. I am worried about the student's drinking more than anything else about him at this time. His problems are the converse of Jon's. He's legal and all, but he turned 18 and is not eligible for any social programs that anyone can think of. When he first arrived here, at age 14, some misguided administrator decided that lack of English is clearly the same as mental retardation and put him back into fourth grade. The result is that at 18 he doesn't have any of the skills high school would have given him, let alone a high school diploma. As with Jon, his situation is a constant worry at the back of my mind.

― ★ ―

As of noon I had met a new Southeast Asian student, her counselor, and the girl's sponsor concerning her program. She's a cute kid, absolutely quiet. I've decided to put the new student into the Junior High after all because the children there are closest to her age and because my associate will be working over there with another sixth grader. I warned the folks at the

Junior High. They're game but nervous, so I ended up listening to the sixth grade counselor's concerns on the phone for half an hour.

---★---

Today a student of mine who had dropped out of school last year reappeared. Completely on his own he showed up for school, still with a chip on his shoulder. I was delighted to see him but did not want him in the very fragile advanced class. I gave him a writing test in which he came out marginal—he probably could make it in the mainstream program if he were willing to work, which is a big "if" for him. After testing him, I talked with his counselor, a new one who knows the student only by reputation, and we decided to mainstream him (and heaven help the mainstream teacher!).

---★---

When the visits to the guidance counselor have to do with planning for college or career, you should monitor closely the advice being given. Many guidance counselors will automatically suggest vocational tracking to language minority students. This advice may fit in well with some families' desire that their children enter the work force as soon as possible, and vocational training may be the best choice for some ESL students, but not for all. Most immigrant families do have a vision of the American

Dream, but they are not sure how to realize it and may depend on cultural traditions or the advice of fellow ethnics. Taking the family situation into account, you should explain the whole postsecondary schooling maze to students: public college, private college, technical school, junior college, 4-year college, full-time studies, part-time studies, scholarships, grants, loans, work-study, and so on. You might have to take students to the colleges for interviews and tours or find ways to pay for standardized tests such as the TOEFL or the SAT. Students will need to be prepared not just in content but in test-taking strategies and control of fear and anxiety. You should work with the guidance department to make sure the students apply for every scholarship for which they are eligible and then help them present their need in applications. Even if the guidance department is good, you still will have to help prepare students for interviews because the whole concept of college is foreign territory for your students. You will have to explain what majors, requirements, and other terms mean and write many recommendations that stress ability, progress, effort, and potential, all the while walking a fine line and keeping a realistic attitude. You will need to be aware of the general population's abilities and to learn which schools have support systems for students from language minority backgrounds.

In spite of the anxiety, you must decide whether you have the right or duty to intervene and to present options to your students that they might never have considered. Though each case will be decided on its own merits, advocacy for your students should be your governing principle whenever possible in dealing with health and guidance issues.

chapter nine

Sponsors: Pros and Cons

FOCUSING QUESTIONS

★ Who are the sponsors of the language minority children?

★ What role do they play in the children's education?

★ How can the ESL teacher call on sponsors for support?

★ What problems can sponsors present for the ESL teacher?

★ How does the ESL teacher handle areas of misunderstanding?

Many immigrant refugees are sponsored by church groups or socially concerned individuals who have a genuine desire to help and, initially at least, are very generous with their money and time. They work tirelessly to find housing, clothing, jobs, and at times automobiles for the families they bring into their communities. Although many sponsors are generally well informed about the sociopolitical situation in the families' countries of origin, few are aware of the day-to-day folkways and mores that govern the lives of the immigrants, at least until they have adopted new cultural patterns.

---★---

I just finished a long phone call from the sponsor of the new Vietnamese family. She's worried that no one speaks English, that the father smokes too much, and that they won't get used to the weather. . . .

---★---

I went to the church to talk to the sponsors about the care and feeding of refugees. At some unspecified time in the future the family they're sponsoring is going to arrive. I was received politely but not terribly enthusiastically. Right now they're worried about beds and jobs.

---★---

It is difficult for some sponsors to understand why the immigrants seem to want to spend all their time with members of their own ethnic group. The newcomers seem reluctant to mix freely with the sponsors in social settings. Gradually, and perhaps not intentionally, the sponsors have less and less contact with the newcomers, rationalizing that the immigrants are now able to make it on their own. When the newcomers suddenly depart for another part of the country, usually an area with a more favorable climate but always one with large numbers of people from their particular ethnic group, the sponsors are crushed. "What did we do wrong?" they ask themselves. They feel somehow cheated, as if the refugees did not express proper gratitude for all the sponsors had done for them.

You will have to be the one who softens the blow for the sponsors while trying to ease the burdens of the refugees. You will soon learn that it is in your interest to meet frequently with the sponsors of your students' families.

For two principal reasons, your job is easier if relations between the families and their sponsors are cordial. First, the most active sponsors tend to visit the schools often. Some may make suggestions about methods and materials they feel are appropriate, and they may encourage mainstream teachers to take advantage of the language minority students in their classrooms by arranging for special presentations and celebrations. If they meet with resistance on any front, they may air their complaints at the next school board meeting. To avoid this unnecessary and most definitely unwanted bad publicity, you should warmly receive visits from sponsors and listen to all their suggestions politely, but subsequently make judicious decisions about which recommendations to implement. As always, diplomacy will be the key to your success with the sponsors.

---★---

*P*enelope Throckmorton came in today to tell me that she and her husband were in the process of sponsoring another Cambodian family. But mainly she came in because she had a few suggestions for me. I'm not opposed to suggestions, even from nonteachers, but I must confess that Penelope puts quite a bit of pressure on me. She always has a lengthy agenda when she comes in—most of which I agree with, fortunately—but I do feel the pressure because I know for certain that if she feels I'm stonewalling, she'll go running to the school board, and who needs that?

I have to deal quite a bit with sponsors. In fact, most of the time I go to them. Many simply drop their families after a while. They seem not to understand the commitment to helping someone adjust to life in the United States or the differences between their values and those of the families. Friendship patterns and family relationships can be hard for them to figure out. When that happens, I put on my hat as cultural ambassador and try to rebuild the bridges. Penelope is a big help because it's hard for folks to say "no" to her.

---★---

*F*ebruary is a month when I feel I've lost it as far as the elementary kids are concerned. Between Valentine's Day, specials, and snow days, plus the vacation at the end of the month, there doesn't seem to be much time for actual language teaching.

Some people came in to observe, and they *would* pick the day the kids were all signing Valentines for the party. Why couldn't they have come on a day when I was doing something that looked like the demonstration lessons in the books? The observers were very kind and said that making Valentines is of course an important part of the culture of the elementary schools, but they missed some of the important aspects of that particular day: that one student's mother, who is on welfare and doesn't have money to spare, managed to get Valentines for both him and his sister; that the boys talked as they worked about the differences between Cambodian and U.S. holidays (U.S. ones are more fun but there's good food at the Cambodian ones); that one student, a nonreader because he isn't ready yet, and another, a nonreader by conviction, both signed all their cards and read some of them, too.

★

The second reason to foster cordial relationships with the sponsoring groups is that they can provide support and services of every kind and will happily do so if properly guided. When ESL students come to school with inadequate clothing, a single phone call to a sponsor will usually produce a veritable barrage of jackets, trousers, or other items of clothing. Another type of support, one that is crucial to the success of your program, is the pressure sponsoring groups can put on recalcitrant school boards. When there is talk, for example, of cutting back on ESL services because of diminishing numbers of language minority students, the sponsors often become very vocal and effective lobbyists in defense of the ESL cause. Because they are often influential members of the community, their opinions carry considerable political weight. If you are wise, you will take advantage of their influence.

--- ★ ---

I stopped by the office and got the enrollment figures. It looks like I'll have 14 students in three schools. That's a lot of work, but at least the administration won't be getting on my case about numbers. Forget about job security; this job will self-destruct if immigration stops. Let's see, do I have any other skills?

--- ★ ---

Sometimes you must chastise the sponsors either for abandoning the newcomers or for behaving toward them in inappropriate ways. At times these contacts are private, but issues are also aired at group meetings, with the sponsored families not present. Being as diplomatic as possible, you should try to instruct the sponsors in your perception of their responsibilities toward the refugee families. You should also deal with their concerns and misunderstandings and attempt to reestablish communication if breakdowns have occurred.

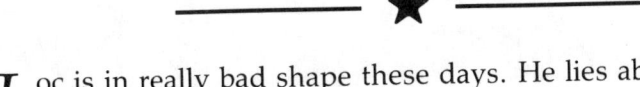

---★---

Loc is in really bad shape these days. He lies about everything and trusts no one. He has shoved a resource room desk against the wall and built a corral around it with cardboard. Though eighth graders store their books and belongings in lockers, he insists upon using "his" desk as a locker and makes sure no one goes near it. Yesterday we heard the report of a psychological evaluation: Loc could straighten out, or he could explode. "Tinderbox" was the word the psychologist used. I called the head of the sponsoring group to see if they could find some counseling for Loc. He told me that Loc just needed to understand the importance of working hard. I mentioned Loc's need for unconditional love, but he said that hard work was the answer. He never had a pair of real shoes until he was 20 years old: "Kids have it too easy today." It was a case of Calvinism versus refugee camp survival skills. Whew!

---★---

You might develop an ambivalent attitude toward sponsors. On the one hand, they perform useful functions: they provide new students for your program, help you meet the day-to-day needs of the immigrants, and support you before the taxpayers. On the negative side, they might interfere with your instructional program and often create extra work for you by frequently requiring your services as cultural interpreter and go-between.

---★---

I've been on the phone for terribly long conversations with various members of the sponsoring group, which is going through all the typical stages such groups do. No, it isn't in the job description, but the sponsors seem to need a shoulder and explainer of cultural differences as much as the refugees do. I figure it all makes my job easier in the end. Besides, the Vietnamese students have parents plus six siblings that the sponsors expect to bring over in the next year. Six more non-English-speaking students would make my job secure for some time to come.

---★---

As an ESL educator, you understand the diversity of cultures, the conflicts produced when cultures come into contact, and the challenges non-English speakers face when trying to cope with U.S. society. Sponsors are good and caring people, but they may not understand as much as you do. You are called upon to include them in your ever-growing pool of audiences to be served.

chapter ten

Function and Identity: I Teach; Therefore, I Am

FOCUSING QUESTIONS

★ Why do ESL teachers often suffer an identity crisis?

★ What aspects of their programs cause ESL teachers to have emotional ups and downs?

★ What is the best way to deal with feelings of frustration and aloneness?

★ What are some of the rewards of being an ESL teacher?

★ What are some typical successes like?

It takes years before the ESL teacher's identity crisis passes definitively. You will arrive on the job, no doubt with a good background and perhaps with prior teaching experience.[1] You will have sailed through the interviews in the hiring process, having answered all questions cogently, but then something will happen to make you wonder exactly where you fit in. It won't be just the attitude and questions of your colleagues, the students' resistance to your attempts to pull them out of their regular classrooms for special instruction, or the efforts of the school board or taxpayer groups to eliminate or undermine your program. The problem will be simply that no one except other ESL professionals—whom you will see at most twice per year—not even your best friends or your family, seems to understand and fully appreciate what you do.

─────────★─────────

*E*very time I meet someone new I have to try to explain what I do. Maybe I should wear my job description on my back. No, that wouldn't help. No one knows what I'm supposed to do. I'm not sure I know either. I just do it.

─────────★─────────

"*Y*ou do what you do." This analysis of the ESL teacher's role, provided by one of my first instructors at the university, has been much on my mind lately. I'm convinced that if someone came in and asked me what I am doing at the high school, they probably wouldn't believe it if I told them. It's all individualized instruction.

I think ESL teachers are in a unique position to broaden the horizons of their students. A student can go through a typical 7-period day with very little opportunity to discuss anything of substance with an adult, yet the adults should be a source of all kinds of information for the students to use in becoming human beings capable of dealing with their surroundings. That happens because teachers in most disciplines feel controlled by the necessity of teaching a certain amount of content. As a result, ESL teachers become the ones who let the students' minds wander as they search for *their* answers. That's a very important role!

I'm not sure other teachers can understand my approach. I

do respect the curriculum guide, and I do attempt to work all the material into my lesson plans, but I cannot predict the order in which I will do so. I used to have nice, neat lesson plans that I adhered to closely, but not anymore. Often I question why I'm in the classroom. I'm usually sure my presence is necessary, but I'm not sure any one particular thing I do is necessary. I watch the students achieving, and I like to think that my presence helps them to achieve, but I'm much less sure of what I'm doing than ever before. Paradoxically, I'm much surer that I'm doing it well than ever before.

Because I wrote my own job description, I was able to define the job and the program to suit my own strengths. Hence the emphasis on home contacts; philosophically I believe in their importance, and I really enjoy visiting the families. I gather they're glad to have me visit, too; the other day one of the women complained that I'd visited so-and-so twice and hadn't been to see *her* for a long time.

Sometimes I feel I've fitted this job to my own specific requirements, probably in the process making myself unfit for any other position and making this position unfit for any other teacher. I've avoided having to answer to anyone else, even my supervisor. The relationship with the administration has developed into one of working *with* it much more than working *for* it. I hadn't realized how much I took this relationship for granted until I had some trouble with the junior high school administrator. My supervisor explained to me that the administrator has trouble with women in positions of authority. Now I work around him and give him the face he needs.

---★---

I forgot to turn in my mileage last month. I probably wouldn't have thought of it if I hadn't been talking to people at the ESL conference. It's a pain, but if I don't do it, I'm out the money. This year I have to make the rounds to only three schools, but they are quite far apart. What I mind is the time I lose from teaching. By the time I pack up my stuff, drag it to the car, load up, drive to the next school, find a parking place, unload, reorganize my materials, and round up my students, I've lost a lot of time. People laugh at me when I tell them that 30 minutes per day per student is about all I can manage, but there's nothing I can do. What do they think I am, a miracle worker?

But I'm off the track. Now, let's see, 120 miles at 24 cents per mile. . . .

---★---

*B*eing an itinerant also makes the job more comfortable for me in a sense. The administration can't catch me for recess duty or bathroom checks, and no one has asked me to substitute teach or take over any duties. I wouldn't mind doing so occasionally, but I don't want to be like the Chapter I teachers, who tend to be plugged into whatever place needs them whether or not they have students scheduled. The principal tried to do that my first year, but no one has since.

My poor family. It is unfortunate that the dinner table has to be the dumping ground for my daily frustrations, but my family doesn't seem to mind it. In fact, I get three custom-made prescriptions to remedy all my ills when the only treatment I want is their sympathetic ears. My supervisor is great, but I can't go running to him every time I bruise my ego; he's swamped as it is. I have found a few teachers who will take the time to listen.

Talking to other teachers is the best solution. I calm down a lot faster when I have the support of other teachers right there on the job only minutes after the crisis erupts than when I let the anger simmer away until the middle of the first course at the dinner table. When I really want to feel I have support, I go to ESL conferences because everyone I tell my troubles to there has 10 stories that make my complaint seem trivial. I do learn from these opportunities to communicate with other ESL professionals. Even if they can't solve what I perceive as my problems, I still feel a certain solidarity with them in the knowledge that I am not suffering alone.

I went to a Silent Way[2] workshop today. I've decided the method just doesn't mesh with my personality and learning style. It occurred to me that teaching systems have great fireworks and flash to get you going when you're already excited anyhow. What we need is fireworks and flash when everybody hits that midlevel slump!

Chapter 10

---★---

*T*hat was a great conference! When I come home bubbly and enthusiastic after a stimulating workshop, my husband always asks me, "How'd it go?" "Great," I respond. "Well, what did you learn?" And I'm stumped. What *did* I learn? I learned . . . I learned once again that I'm OK, that other people face the same frustrations I do, that on the darkest days we all find something to laugh about, and that sharing laughs and frustrations makes me feel renewed. I feel part of something bigger than myself. I feel validated.

"But what did you learn?"

"Well, there's this neat game you can plan with empty cold cereal boxes. You need at least a half dozen different kinds and then you. . . . But, honey, isn't that what you wanted to know?"

---★---

The feeling of not belonging results from your own perceptions. As mentioned, little by little you will manage to win over the people with whom you come into contact, but there will always be new consciousnesses to be raised, and the process will seem never ending. Overlooking the insensitivity of colleagues and supervisors will not be so difficult, but it will be tough when the students go on the attack. When the youngsters seem to want to hurt you after you have done all you can for them, you will ask, "How can it be?"

---★---

*T*he other day I got terribly depressed. It was the 7:30 class that did it. I had spent the weekend putting together a rather neat unit that would include a theme, a grammatical focus, chances for interesting writing, and lots of student interaction. I was looking forward to teaching it, but when I got to school, the whole lesson collapsed under the weight of the students' boredom. I ended up wondering what I was doing there and why. If the devil had appeared in a puff of smoke and offered me a job doing anything that didn't involve students or teaching English, I'd have taken it. No devil appearing, I closed the door to my classroom and cried for a while.

---★---

When these moments of despair come along, having a support network will be very important. In a small ESL program in a public school system, there is generally only one ESL teacher. You will have no departmental structure to facilitate discussion of concerns, and your supervisors will be remote and too busy to listen to daily gripes. You will have to turn to the mainstream classroom teachers as a source of condolence. If you decide to tough it out alone in a self-imposed martyrdom, your energy level will probably decrease until you are no longer effective.

---⭐---

I told a few other teachers how I was feeling, and every one of them helped me. One of them told me, "Stop being so nice. Kick their butts around a bit."

"But maybe it's my fault. Maybe I'm just not as good a teacher as I thought. I don't want to kick their butts if they don't deserve it."

"Oh, they deserve it. If not for that, for something else. Do it, you'll feel better."

Another one, at the elementary school, said, "I don't know how you do it. I couldn't teach those high school students. At least little ones you can overwhelm."

Someone else said, "Don't take it so seriously. Look, you have to laugh or you'll cry in public."

My own children agreed. "Tell them how mad you are and don't let them get away with it. Stop being nice to them. Our teachers aren't nice to us."

The next day I went in and told my students how upset I was at their behavior, and they were amazed that I'd taken it personally. One said, "But yesterday was Monday. I don't wake up until Tuesday."

Another added, "But I was in a bad mood all day. It wasn't about you. I hated all my classes."

---⭐---

For the past few days the students have been great. What I learned from the experience, besides being reminded about adolescent behavior and the need to be tougher than I enjoy, is that we ESL teachers need all the support we can get from teachers in other areas. We don't have a big department of people in our field to share experiences with, so it's up to us to find sympathetic people in other departments. I think I picked the right people to blow off steam to. No one said anything like, "These foreigners should be so grateful for all we do for them," or "What can you expect of *them*?" Instead, the teachers reminded me that my students cause their teacher the same kind of grief that any other students do. Perhaps it is my fault that I let them use me as a shoulder, mommy, and punching bag.

★

Someone asked me the other day, "Why don't you quit the martyr business and get one of the regular ESL jobs?" I've thought about that question a lot, and the answer is, "Because I don't want to." I like the autonomy and the small size of my program. It's easy for me to change things I don't like, to innovate when I have new ideas, and to purchase new materials provided that they don't cost too much. Control over my budget gives me a sense of power. Because there's always more work than I could possibly do, I never have to fill my days with senseless activity—everything I do has value. In how many situations could I go home nearly every day feeling that my efforts have been fruitful?

---- ★ ----

If you cultivate a personal relationship with one or more of your colleagues, chances are you will soon discover that they value your program more than you imagine and that the presumed personal attacks by your students have nothing at all to do with you—except that in your classroom the students may feel freer to express their pent-up anger and frustration. Relieved by this newfound knowledge, you will be able to return to your program with renewed enthusiasm.

You might also find it useful to keep a daybook in which you record the highlights of the day's instructional activities and your thoughts and feelings about the day's events. The writing itself seems to be therapeutic and will help you gain perspective on your experience. You may feel, for instance, that a certain student has been behaving disruptively for a long time. A quick check of the daybook entries might reveal that he has behaved badly only on a few occasions. The calming process can then begin.

---- ★ ----

I'd be a mess without my daybook. Jan has been such a pain recently. It seemed to me that he had been acting up for weeks, but my notes indicate that it was only 3 days—long days, to be sure. It's amazing how slowly time passes when you're hurting. When will I learn that it's *my* problem? I know what the students are going through: a difficult transition to another culture and climate, anomie, often an impossible home life, on top of everything adolescents have to deal with anyway. They're so good at hurting you. How do they learn this? How can they be so sharp when it comes to these sociolinguistic subtleties (to be honest, not always so subtle) and so dull when it comes to the most basic critical thinking skills? That is something to think about. Could we tap this mental capacity in some constructive way?

As for me, I've been hurt many times, and I always get over it. The students have tried to manipulate me for their own amusement or for some other twisted reason. What I'm left with is the pain of seeing very bright students wasted. I don't resent anything they did on purpose, as I did at the beginning of the year. Jan's campaign seemed particularly vicious. Does he really want to destroy me? I thought I was his only anchor in very troubled waters. Maybe that's the problem.

─────── ★ ───────

*A*ll night I dreamed about placing Vietnamese in classes.

Chapter 10

---★---

What kind of teacher am I? For me the only question that counts is, "Are all of my students doing better in school than they were before I worked with them?" There are many variables, and I'm not the only one who helps the students learn, but my specific job is to increase the knowledge and improve the skills of these students. To do so I have to accomplish a myriad of tasks that relate only indirectly to academic instruction. My performance evaluation sheet might look a little unusual to the typical administrator:

Did I visit Kim's home to explain about the field trip?
Did I buy lunch for José, who forgot his lunch box?
Did I translate the school nurse's note for Maria's mother?
Did I spend hours and hours persuading Jon's English teacher that he's not retarded?

Yes, I did. I think I deserve an A!

---★---

I keep thinking about a book that came out at the end of the 1960s: *Teaching as a Subversive Activity* (Postman & Weingartner, 1969). The reason it sticks in my mind is that at times I feel like a subversive agent or at least a devious team member. I don't feel guilty about my actions because I'm sure my supervisor would understand if I explained the reasons behind them, but I know my colleagues would raise their eyebrows if they knew. Sometimes, for instance, I'll spend the entire morning shooting the breeze with my high school class. I think it's great when I can throw away the lesson plan. The students know how to ask a leading question, and then we're off. As long as everyone participates, I think it's fine. It's surely more fun for me.

I get away with these and other things because the administrators feel I am doing them a favor. All they know about ESL is what I've told them. The result is that I can't think of another job where I would have as much freedom. Now that's worth something!

---- ★ ----

June: What a year it's been! I only hope my students have learned as much as I have—a cliché that strikes me with its truth every year at this time. I'll miss them this summer and next fall, even with the excitement of meeting the new ones. I'll miss the ones who have left town, graduated from school, or left the ESL program.

The soft-spoken Cambodian child with the long eyelashes won't be gone, and I'm glad. He is moving along, gently acquiring English steadily and at his own pace. His teacher this year said, "You're so lucky to be able to work with him again next year. I'm really going to miss him. Keep me posted on how he's doing, will you?"

The silly fourth grader was doing so well! It always seems to happen like this: he was at grade level in math, doing fairly well in reading, putting together and occasionally writing stories that had a beginning, a middle, and an end . . . and suddenly in March his family moved out of state to a place with a large Cambodian community. He may never have to speak English again in his life. Mutual friends say that his mother has already decided moving was a big mistake and wishes she could come back here. I hope he's doing OK, but I get depressed whenever I think of it.

José is out of the program. His English came along very quickly. I know language ability and other kinds of intelligence aren't necessarily related, but let's face it, intelligence helps, and José is intelligent. His classroom teacher thought he should leave the program before I thought he was ready. Because his ideas were so good, she simply did not hear the problems in English. I kept him in the program longer than she wanted, but not as long as I would have liked. His father, who is one of those people who sees a stigma in needing ESL, also wanted him out, and clearly I couldn't win. I'd have fought harder, except that I really did think he'd manage without ESL. I saw his mother the other day, and she says he's doing well but won't speak Spanish to her anymore. She's sad about that, but she's in adult ESL classes, so they'll still be able to communicate.

The Taiwanese girl left, too, but she and her best friend in the ESL program have written letters to each other. One of them even called the other long distance. My student reports that her friend is in a place with no ESL program but that she sees a speech therapist once a week. Give me a break! I know the school is doing the best it can, but she doesn't need speech therapy! Sometimes I have fantasies of adopting all of these children and keeping them here, but their parents (and my husband) might object.

The Vietnamese girl is a success story. She worked hard and even made the honor roll. The last time I spoke to her brother, he said he was glad she was getting an education, because "in the United States even women need to go to school." It is still very hard for her because she lacks so much background knowledge, but I've seldom met anyone who loves the process of learning as much as she does. She's in a summer educational program, so it'll be exciting to see what she's achieved by September.

The Cambodian boy graduated from high school. I went to the graduation and took pictures, hugged his girlfriend, and shook his hand.

The Greek girl may have actually gained the most, at least in terms of self-esteem. She went from saying she wanted to work in a factory to announcing the other day, "I know what I want to be. I want to be a lawyer, working in immigration law." I bet she does it, too.

★

How will you feel when the year's end rolls around? You will be relieved that the daily pressure of a tight schedule is behind you for a while; joyful that several students have graduated from the program, either having gone on to college or moved permanently into a mainstream classroom; anxious that the reduction in language minority students could jeopardize your position; and concerned that some of your students will have a difficult summer because of troubles with law enforcement or immigration officials. But most of all you will feel satisfied that, for the umpteenth year, you were called upon to be all things to all people, and you were.

---★---

I spent the day overcome by the annual tide of conflicting emotions. There's something sad and nostalgic about putting books away, cleaning desks, and returning all the students' papers. It makes me feel the way I do when we close up our summer cottage in the fall. Yet what relief I feel knowing that starting tomorrow I won't be here doing frontline duty, constantly in demand from the time of my arrival until my departure. It won't be over completely; I always keep in touch with my families during the summer, especially those who need the most support, and I watch the newspaper carefully to catch any news items having to do with my students. But basically it's over, and I'm ready for a rest.

Notes

1. See Appendix B for an outline of competencies typically required for certification.
2. The Silent Way is a method of language instruction, proposed by Caleb Gattegno (1972), wherein the instructor speaks very little (is "silent") but motivates the students to speak by using charts, rods, and gestures.

postscript

When I think back over the past 20 years, nothing monumental stands out. I guess I'd count up the little things as a measure of my performance. The successes are when a student asks, "What does this mean?" instead of "What means this?" Luckily, successes like that come along fairly frequently, but I don't think the big fancy ones do. When one of my students reads a story at an author's tea, I feel a real sense of parental pride. And when I exit a student from my program, I know I've made a change in the student's life: he can function independently now. It feels good when I help teenagers rise above their family expectations to go to college or pursue an interesting career. The all-time greatest satisfaction has to be seeing a student become a self-directed learner, but most often I have to settle for a flicker of intellectual curiosity—that's nice, too. It is wonderful when students whose cultural background leads them to expect information to be fed to them with a spoon buy into the concept of using critical thinking skills. The flicker of intellectual curiosity is the beginning of the change. It's exciting when I see that flicker, when the students bring up a topic to me.

Sometimes I feel I've helped a student over emotional hurdles. There is rarely any other teacher who has the time to deal with such problems daily. They don't always tell me or anyone else what's on their minds, and when they do I run the risk of becoming too close to them. When they're depressed, it can affect my mood, too.

One student at the high school has been in such a deep depression these days that he's not able to show those flickers. He has a background that doesn't foster intellectual curiosity, let alone critical thinking skills, yet the other day he did manage to pull himself out of the depression. I could see the effort it took him to ask a question, like a hippopotamus getting out of the mud: "Do Americans really think such and so?" I was so glad to hear him ask such a question that I almost ran over and hugged him. Then he retreated into his depression again. But for a moment I saw a definite success.

references

Asher, J. J. (1982). *Learning another language through actions*. Los Gatos, CA: Sky Oaks Productions.

Ashton-Warner, S. (1963). *Teacher*. New York: Simon & Schuster.

Ashton-Warner, S. (1972). *Spearpoint: Teacher in America*. New York: Knopf.

Campbell, R. (1983). *Oh, dear*. New York: Four Winds Press.

Capelle, G., Pavlik, C., & Segal, M. (1985). *I love English*. Englewood Cliffs, NJ: Prentice-Hall.

Costello, P. (1987). *Stories from American business*. Englewood Cliffs, NJ: Prentice-Hall/Regents.

Cummins, J. (1989). *Empowering minority students*. Sacramento, CA: California Association for Bilingual Education.

Gattegno, C. (1972). *Teaching foreign languages in schools: The silent way* (2nd ed.). New York: Educational Solutions.

References

Krashen, S. D. (1982). *Principles and practice in second language acquisition.* Oxford: Pergamon Press.

Krashen, S. D., & Terrell, T. D. (1983). *The Natural Approach.* Hayward, CA: Alemany Press.

Morgan, J., & Rinvoluccri, M. (1987). *Once upon a time: Using stories in the language classroom.* Cambridge: Cambridge University Press.

Olsen, R. (1991). Results of a K-12 and adult ESL enrollment survey—1991. *TESOL Matters, 1*(5), 4.

Postman, N., & Weingartner, C. (1969). *Teaching as a subversive activity.* New York: Delacorte.

Scarcella, R. (1990). *Teaching language minority students in the multicultural classroom.* Englewood Cliffs, NJ: Prentice-Hall/Regents.

Sion, C. (Ed.). (1985). *Recipes for tired teachers: Well-seasoned activities for the ESOL classroom.* Reading, MA: Addison-Wesley.

Smith, F. (1986). *Insult to intelligence.* Portsmouth, NH: Heinemann.

Yorkey, R. (1985). *Talk-a-tivities.* Reading, MA: Addison-Wesley.

appendix a

Parents' Handbook

Dear Parents:

What Is a Handbook?

Every school has a handbook. It tells about the school. This is a special handbook for the parents of children in the ESL program. It explains some of the rules in the official school handbook. It tells about American rules and customs your children will find in school.

School Atmosphere

The U.S. school system may seem strange. It may seem to you that the children play all day. We want children to be happy in school, because happy children learn better than unhappy children. But the children are working hard.

Grades and Papers

Children get grades in all of the subjects they study. Young children may get a smiling face or a sticker on a good paper. This means the teacher likes the paper. Your children will be proud to show you these papers. Some parents put the good papers on the wall or keep them in a folder. Please show your children that you are happy when they get good grades.

Sometimes you may be unhappy with your children's grades. Or perhaps your child is unhappy in school. You should talk with the teacher.

Conferences

Everyone who works with your children wants them to have a good year in school. If you have a question, call the school and make an appointment for a conference with the principal, the teacher, or the ESL teacher. We are happy to talk with you. If there is a problem, we want to help.

Sometimes the parents know there is a problem but are

afraid to bother the teacher. Then maybe the teacher thinks the parents don't care about the children. It is important to call the teacher if you have a question or a problem. Usually a teacher can talk with you at school just before or just after school. The ESL teacher can be there, too, if you want. Sometimes the teacher will ask you to come to school for a conference. The teacher will show you your child's work and books. You will see the room. You will hear the good and bad things your child does. The teacher will tell you how you can help your child. The conference is very important, but it is nothing to worry about.

Attendance

Your child has to go to school every day that the school is open. However, sick children should not go to school. If your child is sick, it is OK to take a day off. If your child is sick or cannot go to school, you must call the school at the time when school starts. But keep the child at home and quiet. Children who are well enough to play outside are well enough to go to school! Sometimes there is a special reason to keep the child at home, such as a visit from a relative from far away or a family trip to another city. But remember that school is the child's job. It is important to go to school.

Clothing

Children in U.S. public schools do not wear uniforms. Informal clothing is allowed, but it should be clean and without holes. Children should wear:
- Underpants and socks
- Shoes
- Pants and shirts
- Skirts and blouses or dresses for girls.

Girls should not wear jewelry that is expensive or that will get in their way during physical education or recess. American girls in elementary school do not wear makeup to school.

Children also need special clothes for cold winter days. They need jackets or sweaters for fall and spring, and an umbrella or a raincoat. In winter, children need to wear boots to school. Sandals or shoes are not good in ice, snow, or mud. The children need boots that fit them. However, they cannot wear boots in school, so they must have shoes to keep in school during the winter. They need warm jackets or coats for winter. They need hats and gloves or mittens and scarves. These are very important, because the weather gets very cold here.

If you cannot afford to buy these clothes, please talk to your ESL teacher, the children's ESL teacher, the adult education coordinator, your sponsor, or your child's teacher. It is always possible to find good, warm clothes to fit your children.

Lost Articles

Sometimes children lose things. Every school has a Lost and Found area. If your child loses something, maybe it is there.

Meals and Snacks

It is important for children to eat breakfast before they go to school. Children learn better if they are not hungry. A good breakfast can be simple.

Children may take a cold lunch to school, or they may get a hot lunch at school. A cold lunch usually has a sandwich, some fruit, and a treat. A hot lunch has some meat, chicken, or fish, a vegetable, some bread or potatoes, and a treat. Children can also get milk or orange juice. Sometimes it is hard for your children to get used to an American school lunch. Some children love it, some children hate it. If there is some American food your child hates or cannot eat, the child does not have to eat it but should tell the ESL teacher.

Some people can have school lunches free or for a low price. Perhaps your children can have the cheaper lunches. The school will send forms home for you to fill out for these reduced-price lunches.

The snack drink is milk or orange juice that the children buy to drink during the recess break. Some children bring a snack from home, too. If your child is always hungry or is growing fast, an extra snack is a good idea. Children like sweet things and potato chips, but fruit or crackers are more healthful.

Sometimes your child's teacher will ask you to send a snack to school for the class.

School Rules

Children know most of the rules. Talk about these rules with your children to make sure they understand.

No fighting with other children. This includes fighting with hands as well as fighting with sticks or throwing things.

No swearing. Sometimes your children may not know that a new word is bad. The teacher will understand the first time a child says a bad word, but the second time, the child will be in trouble!

No throwing rocks or snowballs.

No running in the halls.

No smoking, chewing gum, or being drunk or high in school.

No skipping school or class.

In general, we expect children to be polite and to respect each other, the teachers, and the school and buses.

Discipline

If children cause trouble, they may have to stay after school. They may have to miss recess. They may be suspended: they will not be allowed to come to school for several days. They may be expelled: they will not be allowed to come back to school at all unless changes are made.

Homework

If the teacher gives children homework, they must do it. The children should have a place to work at home (not in front of the TV set!). They need good light and a quiet place to work. They should finish their homework and studying before they play or watch TV, and even before they do housework to help the family.

School Closings

Sometimes there is no school because of a storm. Sometimes school will open late because of a storm or because there is ice on the road. If the weather is bad, listen to the radio in the morning. The person will say something like "Cancellations. There will be no school," or "School will be canceled." If you are not sure, call your friend, your sponsor, or the children's ESL teacher.

Emergencies

If there is an emergency at school, the people at the school will take care of the children. For example, every year the children have fire drills. They practice leaving the school quickly and quietly so that they can escape if there is a fire.

If your child has an emergency, such as an accident, the school nurse will help the child. The secretary will telephone you, and if you are not at home, the secretary will call the other person you put on the card you filled out at the beginning of the year.

School Calendar

There will be no school during holidays and vacations. Also, there are teachers' conferences on one or two days. Children do not go to school on those days, but the parents go to school to talk with the teachers. You will receive a copy of the School Calendar. Please hang it up where you will see it each day.

Holidays and Parties

There are special days almost every month in school. Here are some of the days and how we celebrate them.

October 31: Halloween

This is a special day for children. Children bring costumes to school, and they dress up and have a party. Sometimes the teacher asks parents to send a treat for Halloween. Costumes do not have to be expensive. Sometimes a boy will dress like a ghost, or a girl will dress like a princess. If you cannot think of a costume for your child, ask your sponsor, the child's teacher, or the ESL teacher for help. If you have a beautiful costume from your country, Halloween may not be a good time to wear it. Sometimes children spill juice or ice cream on clothes!

November: Thanksgiving

This is the holiday when Americans remember the Pilgrims, who came to America because the government in England would not let them pray to God the way they wanted to. In school, children make pictures of Pilgrims and Indians. Sometimes they have a play about the first Thanksgiving. Sometimes they have special treats in school.

December 25: Christmas

Outside of school, this is a Christian holiday. In school everyone can participate in activities for Christmas and other winter holidays. Children make presents in school to give to their parents. They make decorations for Christmas trees. In some classes children must get a present for one other child. The present must be cheap—the teacher says how much it can cost. Many children get a Christmas card or a small present for their teacher, too. Then there is a party just before the vacation. Perhaps teachers will ask you to send a treat to school for this party.

January 15: Martin Luther King's Birthday
We honor the memory of this great civil rights leader and peacemaker.

February 14: Valentine's Day
This is a day to say "I love you" to special people in your life. In school, children make or buy Valentine cards to send to each child in class. Again, there is a party with treats for everyone.

February: Presidents' Day
Two presidents, Washington and Lincoln, have their birthdays in February. The children learn about these and other presidents.

March 17: St. Patrick's Day
This is a special day for people whose family came from Ireland, but it is also special for everyone else. Children draw and color pictures of shamrocks and leprechauns, and they all remember to wear something green on this day. If they don't, their friends will pinch them.

Another special day for children is their birthday. In some classes there is a small party, in others there isn't, but this is a day when the parents can send a cake or cookies to school so the class can celebrate.

This may seem like a lot of parties and a lot of cookies.

Usually, the teacher does not ask one family to send more than one treat during the year. Here are some treats you can send:
    a cake
    a package of cookies
    some fruit
    something to drink: a big bottle of juice and some paper cups.
   The best treat is something from your country. Children like to try new foods. It is exciting for your children to share something from their country with their American friends. You can call your child's teacher to ask for ideas or help. If it is impossible to send something you said you would send, call the teacher and say so. The teacher will ask someone else.

Notices From School

Children bring home notes every week. Some of these are not important. They are announcements that are not useful or interesting for your child. Throw these notes away. Other notes are more important. Some tell you something about holidays or special things for the children. Keep these and read them. If you don't understand, ask your sponsor, the ESL teacher, or a friend.
   The most important notes are the ones you must sign and return. These may be about class trips. You must say that it is OK for your child to go on a class trip or do a special thing. Others may be about your child. Sometimes there is a special class for your child, or the teacher may want to talk with you

about your child, or the child can get free or reduced-price lunches. When you sign these notes, tell your child to give them to the teacher! If you don't understand the note, don't sign it. Ask someone to explain it. Then decide if you want to sign it.

appendix b

Linguistic and Cultural Competencies for ESL Teachers[1]

1. *English language:* demonstrated proficiency in spoken and written English
2. *Non-English:* experience in learning a second language and in acquiring a knowledge of its structure
3. *Sociolinguistics:* knowledge of the nature of language and of social, regional, and functional language variation
4. *Development of the English language:* (a) knowledge of the historical development of the English language system and (b) knowledge of current English linguistics (phonological, morphological and syntactic structure)
5. *Language acquisition:* knowledge of the process of acquiring first and subsequent languages and how this process varies with age level
6. *Methods and techniques:* (a) knowledge of the principles and

methods of second language acquisition and (b) ability to apply these principles and methods to various classroom situations and instructional materials

7. *Testing:* ability to design and use instruments that measure student progress and proficiency in a second language and to interpret the results
8. *Evaluation:* ability to evaluate the effectiveness of teaching materials, procedures, and curriculum
9. *Cultural diversity in the United States:* knowledge of the pluralistic nature of U.S. society, its cultural systems, and their interrelationships, with special attention given to Afro-American, Hispanic, and Native American cultures
10. *Cultural experience:* knowledge of at least one other cultural system based, if possible, on firsthand experiences
11. *Sociocultural effects:* an understanding of the effects of sociocultural norms on first and second language learning

Note

1. Adapted from guidelines prepared by the State of New Hampshire Department of Education, Office of Teacher Certification, May 1989, Concord, NH.

appendix c

Glossary of Technical Terms Regarding Services to Limited English Proficient Students in Public Schools[1]

BICS (basic interpersonal communication skills): a term coined by Cummins (see Appendix D) to describe the type of language skills needed for everyday interaction. They are characterized by colloquial grammar and vocabulary and usually limited to the concrete, the here, and the now. If only an informal oral inventory of a student's skills is taken, the student may appear quite proficient in the language measured. See CALP.

CALP (cognitive/academic language proficiency): a term coined by Cummins (see Appendix D) to refer to the language skills needed to be successful in the academic setting. It includes concepts, levels of formality, and classroom jargon that are not typically learned on the playground or in the home setting. A limited English proficient (LEP) student may take 4 to 9 years to reach national grade-level norms of native speakers in all subject areas of language and academic achievement, as measured on standardized tests. This span of time is directly influenced by several factors, including (a) the student's age on arrival in the second language culture, (b) the amount of uninterrupted schooling in the primary or home language, (c) the length of residence in the second language culture, (d) the amount of content area instruction in the primary or home language while learning the second language, and (e) academic aspirations.

Content-based ESL instruction: an approach to second language teaching that uses content area subject matter (literature, social studies, mathematics, science) to teach language. It is believed that attaching meaningful, contextualized concepts to a content area will enhance the second language learning process. This approach also helps second language learners maintain the cognitive structures they may have already developed in the primary or home language. ESL teachers as well as mainstream classroom teachers can use content-based instruction, but it requires special planning to include the language-learning objectives. Before the content lesson, the teacher needs to (a) identify the main ideas and important supporting details, (b) identify important vocabulary, (c) rewrite the main idea in language the LEP student is able to understand, (d) plan nonverbal strategies for teaching the concept, (e) teach content area reading strategies, and (f) evaluate the learning taking place. The teacher may also want to investigate the appropriateness of using a content area textbook with LEP students.

English as a second language (ESL): an umbrella term used to describe any program for nonnative speakers of English. Many ESL students are placed in mainstream classrooms for most of the day and receive extra instruction in English. This extra help is based on a special curriculum designed to teach ESL. The non-English home language may or may not be used in conjunction with ESL instruction. ESL is often taught through "pull-out" classes.

Exit criteria: standards developed by educators to define when an LEP student has made enough progress in the ESL program to be able to function at grade level in the mainstream classroom. Policy and procedures should be clearly articulated, and practices should support such policy. Students should not be removed from special language programs without a formal evaluation.

Grade equivalent: one way to describe the grade placement of a student based on his or her test performance. Although grade equivalents can be used to describe general performance, they are often misleading and should be reported with caution. (A grade equivalent of 7.0 by a fifth grade student *does not* mean that the student can do seventh grade work.) In addition, most grade equivalents are estimates.

Limited English proficient (LEP): a term used to describe students with a primary language other than English who have English language deficiencies. The opportunity for them to participate effectively in school may be denied when English is the exclusive language of instruction.

Natural Approach: Based on the writings of Stephen Krashen and Tracey Terrell (see Appendix D), the Natural Approach stresses simplified speech and visual or physical clues to help students comprehend second language input. Teachers focus on meaningful and interesting communication, resist the impulse to correct students' errors overtly, and avoid pressuring children to produce speech in the second language before they are ready.

The Natural Approach uses instructional techniques that facilitate the natural process of acquiring a language. Teachers must provide comprehensible input to language learners that must contain a message the learner needs. In addition, second language acquisition requires an environment as free as possible from anxiety. An initial silent period in which students are developing the receptive skill of listening and the teacher is providing meaningful messages in modified speech is a prerequisite to speech production by students. The teacher accepts all attempts by the learners to communicate, even if expressed incorrectly or in the first language. The teacher expands on but does not translate students' incorrect or incomplete utterances, in a natural extension of two-way communication. These expansions provide additional input. Speech thus emerges but is not specifically taught. Drilling has no place in this approach because it forces learners to speak before they are ready and serves no real communicative purpose.

Sheltered English: simplified English used to teach English and content at the same time. It is also called alternate immersion, in which children receive instruction geared to their level of English proficiency, usually at first in subjects that are less language intensive, such as mathematics, and later in subjects that are more so, such as social studies.

Standardized achievement tests: tests that sample a student's present level of learning across a range of general skill areas. The content is typically related to formal school learning experiences, and because the intent is to sort and rank students, the tests cover a wide range of topic areas. The norms for a standardized achievement test show how "typical" mainstreamed students performed and can be used as a basis for determining how students in a program are progressing in relation to their mainstream peers.

Because they measure school learning, standardized achievement tests can provide some very useful information for those who work with LEP students. The results of the tests can provide a picture of overall progress over time, identify skills that students have learned and those that still need to be taught, and help determine whether students are ready to move into the mainstream. Once students have the language skills necessary to take a standardized achievement test, the results can be used to ensure that students in a program are helped to develop skills comparable to those of their mainstream, monolingual peers.

Total Physical Response (TPR): proposed by Asher (see Appendix D) as a method paralleling first language acquisition sequences. In Asher's view, the second language learner should approach language as the young child does, by listening for most of the first year of life and speaking only when ready. The teacher gives commands in the new language; the teacher and then the students act them out. As the commands become increasingly more complex, visual aids are used to enrich vocabulary. Students begin to speak when they feel ready to do so, and the flow of communication is not interrupted by error correction. Only during the last few minutes of class are students permitted to ask questions in their native language. This approach has been used to teach a variety of languages and has been the subject of experimental studies that show impressive language gain and retention and transfer of oral skills to reading and writing.

Note

1. Adapted from the glossary prepared by Marc J. R. Brenman, Division Director, Office for Civil Rights, U.S. Department of Education, Region I, Boston, MA, October 1989.

appendix d

Bibliography

Recommended for Classroom Use

Elementary Level
Campbell, R. (1983). *Oh, dear*. New York: Four Winds Press.

Capelle, G., Pavlik, C., & Segal, M. (1985). *I love English* (Levels 1–4). Englewood Cliffs, NJ: Prentice-Hall/Regents.

Claire, E. (1990). *ESL teacher's activities kit*. West Nyack, NY: Center for Applied Research in Education.

Claire, E. (1990). *ESL teacher's holiday activities kit*. West Nyack, NY: Center for Applied Research in Education.

Frauman-Prickel, M., & Takahashi, N. (1985). *Action English pictures*. Hayward, CA: Alemany Press.

Graham, C. (1979). *Jazz chants for children*. New York: Oxford University Press.

Graham, C. (1986). *Small talk*. New York: Oxford University Press.

Hudelson, S., & Graham, C. (1984). *Hopscotch* (basal series for ages 5–10). Englewood Cliffs, NJ: Prentice-Hall.

Linfield, T. (Ed.). (1982). *Reach out* (Books 1–5, elementary basal). New York: Macmillan.

Linse, C. (1983). *The children's response*. Hayward, CA: Alemany Press.

Palmer, A. S., Rogers, T. S., & Olsen, J. W.-B. (1985). *Back and forth: Pair activities for language development*. Hayward, CA: Alemany Press.

Parnell, E. C. (1988). *The new Oxford picture dictionary*. New York: Oxford University Press.

Romijn, E., & Seely, C. (1985). *Live action English*. Hayward, CA: Alemany Press.

Secondary Level

Alexander, L. G., & Cornelius, E. T. (1978). *Comp: Exercises in comprehensive and composition*. White Plains, NY: Longman.

Brooks, G., & Withrow, J. (1988). *10 steps: Controlled composition for beginning and intermediate language development*. Hayward, CA: Alemany Press.

Costello, P. (1987). *Stories from American business*. Englewood Cliffs, NJ: Prentice-Hall.

Graham, C. (1978). *Jazz chants*. New York: Oxford University Press.

Jones, L., & Kimbrough, V. (1987). *Great ideas* (with tape). Cambridge: Cambridge University Press.

Kuntz, L. (1988). *The new arrival*. Hayward, CA: Alemany Press.

Kuntz, L. A. (1988). *26 steps: Controlled composition for intermediate and advanced language development*. Hayward, CA: Alemany Press.

Ladousse, G. P. (1983). *Speaking personally: Quizzes and questionnaires for fluency practice*. Cambridge: Cambridge University Press.

Molinsky, S. J., & Bliss, B. (1990). *Side by side* (basal series for secondary and adult). Englewood Cliffs, NJ: Prentice-Hall.

Morgan, J., & Rinvoluccri, M. (1987). *Once upon a time: Using stories in the language classroom*. Cambridge: Cambridge University Press.

Noone, L. (1986). *The ability to risk: Reading skills for beginning students of ESL*. Englewood Cliffs, NJ: Prentice-Hall/Regents.

Rinvoluccri, M. (1984). *Grammar games*. Cambridge: Cambridge University Press.

Sion, C. (Ed.). (1985). *Recipes for tired teachers: Well-seasoned activities for the ESOL classroom*. Reading, MA: Addison-Wesley.

Yorkey, R. (1985). *Talk-a-tivities*. Reading, MA: Addison-Wesley.

Teacher Resources

Allen, E. D., & Valette, R. M. (1977). *Classroom techniques: Foreign languages and English as a second language*. New York: Harcourt Brace Jovanovich.

Asher, J. J. (1982). *Learning another language through actions*. Los Gatos, CA: Sky Oaks Productions.

Ashton-Warner, S. (1963). *Teacher*. New York: Simon & Schuster.

Calkins, L. (1986). *The art of teaching writing*. Portsmouth, NH: Heinemann.

Cummins, J. (1989). *Empowering minority students*. Sacramento, CA: California Association for Bilingual Education.

Curran, C. A. (1976). *Counseling-learning in second languages*. Apple River, IL: Apple River Press.

Curran, C. A. (1978). *Understanding*. Apple River, IL: Apple River Press.

Dixon, C. N., & Nessel, D. (1983). *Language experience approach to reading and writing: LEA for ESL*. Hayward, CA: Alemany Press.

Fulwiler, T. (Ed.). (1987). *The journal book*. Portsmouth, NH: Heinemann.

Gattegno, C. (1972). *Teaching foreign languages in schools: The silent way* (2nd ed.). New York: Educational Solutions.

Hall, E. T. (1977). *Beyond culture*. Garden City, NJ: Anchor Press/Doubleday.

Krashen, S. D. (1982). *Principles and practices in second language acquisition*. Oxford: Pergamon Press.

Krashen, S. D., & Terrell, T. D. (1983). *The natural approach*. Hayward, CA: Alemany Press.

Postman, N., & Weingartner, C. (1969). *Teaching as a subversive activity*. New York: Delacorte.

Richard-Amato, P., & Snow, M. A. (1992). *The multicultural classroom: Readings for content-area teachers* (extensive bibliography). White Plains, NY: Longman.

Saville-Troike, M. (1976). *Foundations for teaching English as a second language*. Englewood Cliffs, NJ: Prentice-Hall.

Scarcella, R. (1990). *Teaching language minority students in the multicultural classroom*. Englewood Cliffs, NJ: Prentice-Hall/Regents.

Smith, F. (1986). *Insult to intelligence*. Portsmouth, NH: Heinemann.

Stevick, E. W. (1976). *Memory, meaning, and method*. Rowley, MA: Newbury House.

about the authors

Donald N. Flemming, Professor of Modern Languages at Keene State College of the University System of New Hampshire, holds a PhD in Hispanic Linguistics from the University of Massachusetts in Amherst. He has been active in the ESL field since 1973. Dr. Flemming has taught ESL in an adult basic education program, has served extensively as a teacher trainer and consultant for public school ESL personnel, received a grant from the U.S. Department of Education to develop a model program for vocational ESL, and has served in many leadership roles in the regional affiliate of TESOL, including president and newsletter editor. He has published many articles and reviews on ESL topics.

Lucie C. Germer teaches ESL to grades K–12 for the Keene, New Hampshire, school system. She holds a PhD in Cultural

Anthropology from the University of Utah. Dr. Germer has extensive international experience, having lived in nine foreign countries, and has a taught ESL in a wide variety of settings both in the United States and abroad. She has presented numerous workshops for ESL teachers and has written articles for the Northern New England TESOL newsletter. She currently serves as President of the Northern New England TESOL affiliate.

Christiane Kelley, an ESL teacher in the Alexandria, Virginia, school district, holds an MA in TESL from Teachers College, Columbia University. She has a strong background in tests and measurement, having worked in this area for some 10 years, and has extensive experience as an ESL teacher in the public schools at levels K–12. Ms. Kelley has presented workshops on a number of ESL-related topics and has served as editor and writer for a number of publications.

Also available from TESOL

A New Decade of Language Testing Research: Selected Papers From the 1990 Language Testing Research Colloguium
Dan Douglas and Carol Chapelle, Editors

A World of Books: An Annotated Reading List for ESL/EFL Students
Dorothy S. Brown

Children and ESL: Integrating Perspectives
Pat Rigg and D. Scott Enright, Editors

Coherence in Writing: Research and Pedagogical Perspectives
Ulla Connor and Ann Johns, Editors

Current Perspectives on Pronunciation: Practices Anchored in Theory
Joan Morley, Editor

Dialogue Journal Writing with Nonnative English Speakers: A Handbook for Teachers
Joy Kreeft Peyton and Leslee Reed

Dialogue Journal Writing with Nonnative English Speakers: An Instructional Packet for Teachers and Workshop Leaders
Joy Kreeft Peyton and Jana Staton

Directory of Professional Preparation Programs in TESOL in the United States, 1992–1994

Diversity as Resource: Redefining Cultural Literacy
Denise E. Murray, Editor

Ending Remediation: Linking ESL and Content in Higher Education
Sarah Benesch, Editor

Research in Reading in English as a Second Language
Joanne Devine, Patricia L. Carrell, and David E. Eskey, Editors

Selected Articles from the TESOL Newsletter: 1966–1983
John F. Haskell, Editor

Students and Teachers Writing Together: Perspectives on Journal Writing
Joy Kreeft Peyton, Editor

Video in Second Language Teaching: Using, Selecting, and Producing Video for the Classroom
Susan Stempleski and Paul Arcario, Editors

For more information, contact

Teachers of **E**nglish to **S**peakers of **O**ther **L**anguages, Inc.
1600 Cameron Street, Suite 300
Alexandria, Virginia 22314 USA
Tel 703-836-0774 ● Fax 703-836-7864